EQUAL OPPORTUNITIES

EQUAL OPPORTUNITIES

A Practical Handbook

Gill Taylor

The Industrial Society

First published in 1994 by
The Industrial Society
Robert Hyde House
48 Bryanston Square
London W1H 7LN
Telephone: 071–262 2401

© The Industrial Society 1994

ISBN 1 85835 175 8

**British Library Cataloguing-in-Publication Data.
A catalogue record for this book is available from the
British Library**

All rights reserved. No part of this publication may be reproduced, stored in an retrieval system or transmitted, in any form or by any means, electronic, mechanical, photocopying, recording and/or otherwise without the prior written permission of the publishers. This book may not be lent, resold, hired out or otherwise disposed of by way of trade in any form, binding or cover other than that in which it is published, without prior consent of the publishers.

Typeset by: The Midlands Book Typesetting Company, Loughborough
Printed by: Lavenham Press
Cover design: Integra Communications

CONTENTS

List of abbreviations

Introduction — 1
Who should use this book? — 1
Why develop equal opportunities management skills? — 2
    Business efficiency
    Quality management
    The labour market
    Legal considerations
    Human rights and social justice
Implications — 5
The positive benefits to business — 6
Structure of the handbook — 7
    Chapter format

1 Equality Targets and Monitoring — 9
1.1 **Setting equality targets** — 11
    Action summary
1.2 **Positive action** — 14
    Affirmative action
    Quotas for people with disabilities
    Genuine Occupational Qualification
    Removing barriers
    Action summary
1.3 **Monitoring** — 22
    What to monitor
    How to monitor
    Analysis
    Action summary
1.4 **Action summary** — 30
1.5 **Legal summary** — 31

2 Recruitment — 32
2.1 **Vacancy analysis** — 34
    Information collection

Flexible ways of working
Action summary
2.2 **The recruitment process** 38
Responsibility for co-ordination and consultation
The job description
The person specification
Recruitment methods
Advertising
The design of key documents
Administration
Action summary
2.3 **Action summary** 69
2.4 **Legal summary** 72

3 **Selection** 73
3.1 **Principles of equality selection** 75
Prejudice
Stereotyping
Unequal treatment
Gut reactions
Action summary
3.2 **Screening and shortlisting** 81
Screening
Why shortlist?
Shortlisting panels
Procedures for shortlisting
Action summary
3.3 **Assessment methods** 94
Selection methods
Selection tests
Types of tests
Using selection tests
Interviews
Action summary

3.4	**The interviewing procedure**	107
	The aim	
	Interviews for people with disabilities	
	Practicalities	
	Panel preparation	
	Asking the questions	
	Action summary	
3.5	**Action summary**	120
3.6	**Legal summary**	121
4	**Deciding on and Appointing New Staff**	**123**
4.1	**Reaching a decision**	125
	Responsibility for and timing of decision on an appointment	
	Deciding on the best person	
	Action summary	
4.2	**References and other checks**	130
	References	
	Police checks	
	Medical examination	
	Qualification checks	
	Action summary	
4.3	**Offer of appointment**	140
	The offer letter	
	Written terms and conditions	
	Action summary	
4.4	**Induction**	145
	Format	
	Induction for a person with a disability	
	Action summary	
4.5	**Probation**	149
	Action summary	
4.6	**Action summary**	157
4.7	**Legal summary**	158

5	**Employment**	161
5.1	**Contractual issues**	163
	Issues for different groups of employees	
	Contract terms and conditions	
	Action summary	
5.2	**Staff development**	176
	Support, supervision and appraisal	
	Promotions, transfers, regrading, redeployment	
	Action summary	
5.3	**Harassment**	189
	What is harassment?	
	But it doesn't happen here!	
	Developing a policy on harassment	
	Employee's action in cases of harassment	
	Procedures	
	Action summary	
5.4	**Disciplinary, grievance and dismissal procedures**	201
	General guidelines	
	Grievance procedures	
	Disciplinary procedures	
	Dismissal	
	Appeal procedures	
	Action summary	
5.5	**Action summary**	210
5.6	**Legal summary**	213
6	**Flexible Working**	216
6.1	**Management of flexible working**	218
	Why offer flexible terms?	
	Strategy and planning	
	Access	
6.2	**Forms of flexible working**	222
	Job sharing and job splitting	
	Part-time employment	
	Working from home or teleworking	

6.3	**Action summary**	241
6.4	**Legal summary**	242
7	**The Law**	**244**
7.1	**The laws covered**	245
7.2	**People with disabilities**	246
	Disabled Persons Employment Act 1944 and 1958 and (NI) Acts 1945 and 1960	
	The Companies (Directors' Report) (Employment of Disabled Persons) Regulations 1980	
	Code of Good Practice	
	Grants to employers of people with disabilities	
7.3	**Black and ethnic minority people**	250
	Race Relations Act 1976	
	The Commission for Racial Equality	
	Definitions of discrimination	
	CRE Code of Practice	
7.4	**Sex discrimination**	254
	The Equal Pay Act 1970	
	The Sex Discrimination Act 1975	
	The Equal Opportunities Commission	
7.5	**Ex-offenders**	258
	Rehabilitation of Offenders Act 1974 and Exemptions Order 1975; Rehabilitation of Offenders (NI) Order 1978 and Exceptions Order 1979	
7.6	**Trade unionists**	262
	Trade Union and Labour Relations (Consolidation) Act 1992, s137; Employment Act 1990	
7.7	**Religious belief or political opinion (Northern Ireland)**	263
	Fair Employment (NI) Act 1976 and 1989 and Fair Employment Monitoring Regulations (NI) 1989	
7.8	**Terms and Conditions of Employment**	268
	Employment Protection (Consolidation) Act 1978 as amended	
	Contracts of Employment and Redundancy Payments Act (NI) as amended 1965	

Employment Act 1990
Trade Union (Consolidation) Act 1992
Trade Union Reform and Employment Rights Act 1993
Medical records
References
7.9 **Data protection** 273
Data Protection Act 1984
7.10 **EC Directives and ECJ decisions** 274
Pregnant women
Forthcoming EC legislation
Challenging prejudice
7.11 **Action Summary** 277

8 **Resources** 279
8.1 **Reference section** 279
Equal opportunities
Chapter 1: Equality targets, positive action and monitoring
Chapters 2–4: Recruitment, selection and appointment
Chapter 5: Employment — contract terms and conditions
Chapter 6: Flexible working
Chapter 7: The law
8.2 **Address section** 289
General resourcing organisations
Equal opportunities — general
People with disabilities
People of different religions and political persuasions in Northern Ireland
Women
Lesbian and gay people
Ex-offenders
AIDS and HIV resource organisations
The law and employment issues
Job sharing

ABBREVIATIONS

ACAS	Advice, Conciliation and Arbitration Service
AIDS	Acquired Immune Deficiency syndrome
CBI	Confederation of British Industry
CRE	Commission for Racial Equality
EAT	Employment Appeals Tribunal
EC	European Community
ECJ	European Court of Justice
ED	Employment Department
EOC	Equal Opportunities Commission
FEA	Fair Employment Act
FEC	Fair Employment Commission
GLC	Greater London Council
GOQ	Genuine Occupational Qualification
HIV	Human Immunodeficiency Virus
IPM	Institute of Personnel Management
IRS	Industrial Relations Services
NI	Northern Ireland
PACT	Placing, Assessment and Counselling Team
RRA	Race Relations Act
s	section of an Act of Parliament
SDA	Sex Discrimination Act
SMP	Statutory Maternity Pay
SSP	Statutory Sick Pay
TURER	Trade Union Reform and Employment Rights Act

INTRODUCTION

All companies want to be competitive and all companies want to have high-quality standards. An important aspect of this is an involved, motivated and high-quality workforce. To get a high standard of workers you need to be absolutely sure that you are getting the best people for the job based on their ability to perform, their talent, and their potential to develop.

This handbook will tell you how to do that through implementing the best equal opportunities standards in recruitment, selection and employment. It is aimed primarily at line managers and personnel managers, who are at the forefront of recruitment, selection and employment decisions — people who may make strategic decisions every day and who need an accessible guide to achieving a productive, diverse and committed workforce. The handbook is practical and detailed, with clear action points. It incorporates all the latest law (including the Trade Union Reform and Employment Rights Act, TURER) and legal cases, and explains concepts clearly.

WHO SHOULD USE THIS BOOK

Are you interested in:

- knowing the lawful parameters to action?
- working out the best equal opportunities practice?
- recruiting the best team possible?
- working in partnership with the personnel department?
- implementing quality targets?
- employing a committed and diverse team?
- helping the team work well together?

If you can answer Yes to one or more of the above then you need the Handbook.

Implementing an equal opportunities strategy successfully means that the whole organisation must recognise ownership of it as a good business practice that benefits all employees and customers.

Top management need to be committed, to support and to reinforce;
Personnel management develop the policies, planning and special knowledge;
Line management are key implementers.

We recognise that line managers, a crucial link in this chain, have been somewhat neglected by the literature. This Handbook will develop and enhance your skills and abilities and help you to be more effective and efficient.

WHY DEVELOP EQUAL OPPORTUNITIES MANAGEMENT SKILLS?

There are five main reasons:

- business efficiency
- quality management
- the labour market
- legal considerations
- human rights and social justice

BUSINESS EFFICIENCY

Launching the Equality Agenda in 1991, Joanna Foster, the then chair of the Equal Opportunities Commission (EOC), recognised the importance of the economic case:

> 'Equal opportunities in the 1990s is about economic efficiency and social justice.'

She echoes Baroness Seear who said in 1981:

> 'But if people, who on merit would get a particular job are not appointed for some irrelevant reason, the job being filled by a less suitable person, the enterprise is that much poorer.
> **Since it is management's contribution to make the most effective use of all available resources, material and human, it is clearly part of their job to see that such a waste of abilities is avoided.'**

A key element of business efficiency is getting the best person for the job, which implies using fair and non-discriminatory recruitment and selection practices. You will not be rejecting people for reasons that have nothing to do with their potential to contribute to your organisation. Keeping an open mind about who can do what will mean a more efficient business.

QUALITY MANAGEMENT

Quality management emphasises the setting of high standards for continuous improvements in production, service delivery and customer care, which in turn rely on high standards of performance from workers. **Equal opportunities management** techniques emphasise and help to ensure this outcome by:

- overcoming barriers and blocks to people because of equality issues, such as harassment, prejudice and stereotyping;
- encouraging participation in decision-making;

- stressing the development of teams and team contributions to the work;
- treating people as individuals, with skills that managers can enhance.

THE LABOUR MARKET

The workforce is changing and shrinking. From the mid 1990s there will be a 25% reduction in entry-level workers compared to the 1980s. By the year 2000 there will be about 2.3 million more people aged 25–64 in the workforce and about 1.3 million fewer aged under 25. There will also be a higher percentage of women and black people in the workforce. In the United States, the Department of Labor predicts that, by 2000, 75–85% of people entering the workforce will be women and people from minority ethnic groups.

In spite of the recession in the early 1990s, the underlying demographic trend means that the workforce is changing rapidly and will continue to do so over the coming decades. Employers need a strategic approach to keep a competitive edge. This will mean an even greater reliance on equal opportunities management techniques to attract and retain the best workers.

LEGAL CONSIDERATIONS

The lawful framework is in place on the statute books and needs to be adhered to unless you wish to incur large penalties and adverse publicity. EC directives will further increase this legal framework in the near future.

It is your responsibility to make sure that your recruitment and employment practices comply

with the law and that the service you provide is available to all members of the community.

HUMAN RIGHTS AND SOCIAL JUSTICE

Moral and ethical imperatives still apply as part of an agenda for implementing equal opportunities. Companies that are concerned about their image, and genuinely wish to encourage a stable society in the long term, will care about implementing equal opportunities as a good long-term business strategy.

IMPLICATIONS

Organisations that want the most productive workforce are going to have to put aside all the old ideas about recruiting and employing 'people like us'. They will have to compete for:

- women
- people from different minority ethnic groups
- people with disabilities
- people of different ages
- people with AIDS or who are HIV positive
- lesbians or gay men
- people with a criminal record
- people of different religions or political beliefs
- people with different family or caring responsibilities
- people of different nationalities

- people of different skin colours
- people who are members of a trade union
- women who are pregnant

Once you have recruited them, there will also be a need to develop and retain this new diverse workforce. This poses new challenges for managers who may not be used to managing a multicultural and diverse workforce to get the best teamwork and productivity.

THE POSITIVE BENEFITS TO BUSINESS

- a diverse workforce offering a rich mix of skills and experience
- flexible working arrangements to meet business needs
- a stable, skilled, well-trained workforce, who return to work after breaks from employment
- retention of the best people by ensuring their needs are fully taken into account
- increased productivity by raising motivation and commitment
- increased profitability by reducing staff turnover and recruitment costs
- managing change by attracting people with new and different ways of thinking
- creating a working environment where total quality can take root
- recruiting the best talent from the available workforce

- a high-profile ethical stand, which is good for the organisation's image
- anticipating and meeting the changing needs of customers

STRUCTURE OF THE HANDBOOK

The handbook covers equal opportunities techniques that increase the effectiveness of management practices to gain the positive benefits outlined above. It is divided into four main parts:

	Chapter
Setting equality targets and monitoring	1
Recruitment	2
Selection	3
Appointment	4
Employment	5
Flexible working	6
The law	7
Resources	8

The law chapter includes the Fair Employment Act and explains which laws refer to England and which to Northern Ireland.

The Handbook is relevant, applicable and legally accurate for England and Northern Ireland as of 31 November 1993.

CHAPTER FORMAT

Each chapter is laid out in the same format for ease of use:

Introduction
Key concepts
Questions answered
Contents
Chapter action summary
Legal summary

EQUALITY TARGETS AND MONITORING

A key aspect of equality management is to set *equality targets* for recruitment and selection on an annual basis and to take *positive and affirmative action* to achieve them. This will make sure that you are implementing equal opportunities management as fully as possible, and speed up the attainment of your recruitment and employment goals. The aim of *positive action* is to encourage and help black and ethnic minority people, women and people with disabilities to apply for work in which they have been underrepresented in the past, and to get access to training to help them qualify for jobs and promotion.

KEY CONCEPTS

- setting equality targets
- positive action
- affirmative action
- quotas
- genuine Occupational Qualification
- monitoring

QUESTIONS ANSWERED

- what is an equality target?
- what is affirmative action?
- what is positive action? Is it the same as positive discrimination or reverse discrimination?
- how many people with disabilities do I have to employ?
- how do I set up effective monitoring systems?
- what records do I have to keep and for how long?

CONTENTS

1: **Setting equality targets**
   Northern Ireland
   Action summary
2: **Positive action**
   What positive action is NOT
   Why take positive action?
   Affirmative action
   Quotas for people with disabilities
   Genuine occupational qualification
   Removing barriers
   Age
   HIV and AIDS
   People with disabilities
   Action summary
3: **Monitoring**
   What to monitor
   Monitoring people of different ethnic origins
   Monitoring women
   Monitoring people with disabilities
   Monitoring religion (Northern Ireland)
   Monitoring age
   Monitoring lesbians and gay men
   How to monitor
   The current workforce
   Application forms
   Selection and appointment
   Promotion and training
   Analysis
   Action summary
4: **Action summary**
5: **Legal summary**

1.1 SETTING EQUALITY TARGETS

An equality target is:

A forecast or estimate of the percentage of ethnic minority employees, women or people with disabilities that employers aim to have in their workforce by a specified date.

The target may be expressed either as a percentage of the total workforce or of all recruits to particular job or grades or as an improvement to the current percentage of such employees.

If you decide to adopt targets, then you need a monitoring system to find out the current profile of job applicants and employees at various levels in the organisation. In this way the employers can identify areas of underrepresentation that need closer study and action to address them. Remember that some potential applicants could be put off by the wording of an advertisement and might not bother to apply.

Setting targets and taking positive action measures are strategies recommended by the Commission for Racial Equality Code of Practice and the Equal Opportunities Commission Code of Practice.

Targets are not quotas nor do they imply reverse or positive discrimination, both of which are unlawful.

A quota is *where you require that a certain percentage of jobs must be reserved for people from a particular racial group*. This is unlawful.
(However, you are allowed to have a quota for people with disabilities. See p. 17 below.)

Reverse or positive discrimination *is the process where you recruit from one sex or from one racial group to even up the numbers in the workforce*. This is unlawful.

If effective steps are taken under positive action and by removing direct and indirect discrimination, there is no reason why the percentage of black and ethnic minority people, women and employees with disabilities should not be significantly increased in many organisations.

NORTHERN IRELAND

In Northern Ireland, the Fair Employment Act (FEA) *requires that you must*:

1. Review recruitment practices

    All registered employers MUST review their recruitment, training and promotion practices. The purpose is to see if there is fair participation in their workforce and whether affirmative action measures are required.

2. Monitor the workforce:

    All private sector firms of 10 or more employees MUST register with the Fair Employment Commission.

    All registered firms MUST submit an annual monitoring return to the Fair Employment Commission (FEC) showing the religious composition of their workforce.

    All public sector employers and private sector employers

of over 250 workers MUST submit annual returns on job applications.
3. Set goals and timetables.
4. Take affirmative action measures (see below).

ACTION SUMMARY

- identify the catchment areas from which your employees and current job applicants come or could come for a particular type of job

- estimate the main proportions of men, women, people with disabilities and ethnic minorities available for different types of work

- review your figures against the results of the research

- set short- and long-term targets for job applicants and recruitment, training and promotion

When recruiting:

Do

- contact the personnel department or monitoring officer and find out what positive action measures you can take for that particular post or group of posts

- consult your department's equality targets for the year

- monitor the results

- review progress against targets annually

But remember, Don't

- set quotas (except for people with disabilities)

- operate any 'reverse discrimination' measures

1.2 POSITIVE ACTION

The Commission for Racial Equality (CRE) and the Equal Opportunities Commission (EOC) state that POSITIVE ACTION means:

- recognising and developing potential that has not been used because of past discrimination and disadvantage

- encouraging applications from suitable black and ethnic minority people and women so that they can be considered equally with other candidates

- providing training for black and ethnic minority people and women so that they can become equally qualified with other candidates

Training bodies can provide training for members of a particular racial group, opportunities for training for particular work, or encouragement to take advantage of opportunities for doing that work when they have been underrepresented in that work at any time within the previous 12 months.

For example:
Educational and training institutions in the West Midlands are joining forces in 1993 to encourage students from ethnic minorities to enter teaching training courses.

Employers can provide training for their employees of a particular racial group or sex to take advantage of opportunities for work in which they have been underrepresented in the past 12 months; and in Northern Ireland provide targeted training to secure fair participation.

EQUALITY TARGETS AND MONITORING

For example
The Civil Service has run a week-long management development course for ethnic minority executive and higher executive staff to enable them to compete more effectively for promotions.

- encouraging applications from people with disabilities where they represent under 3% of the workforce

In addition, there are also certain circumstances in which black and ethnic minority people and women can be specifically recruited to a post. See the section on 'Genuine Occupational Qualification' below.

Further examples of possible action are contained in the booklet on 'Positive Action and Equal Opportunity in Employment' by the CRE.

WHAT POSITIVE ACTION IS NOT

- it is NOT selecting a black or ethnic minority person or a woman irrespective of merit to give an organisation a good image

- it is NOT selecting a person simply because they are black or from an ethnic minority to create a racial balance

- it is NOT selecting a woman simply because she is a woman to achieve a balance of the sexes

It is unlawful to shortlist only women or ethnic minority people from your pool of applicants, regardless of merit, even if you genuinely want to achieve a balance of people at work.

It is also unlawful to select a person for a job on the basis of their experience of being black or being a woman to help you develop your equal opportunities policies.

WHY TAKE POSITIVE ACTION?

Positive action in **race equality** is necessary because:

- the effects of racism in society, in education, and in access to housing and employment have resulted in black and ethnic minority people generally being less able to compete equally with the white population

- even if selection criteria and appointment procedures were all changed overnight to remove direct and indirect discrimination, it would take many years to redress the effects of this past discrimination

- positive action seeks to put black and ethnic minority people onto a fair footing with white people so that they can compete equally for jobs

Positive action for **women** is necessary because:

- the majority of women are concentrated in a limited range of professions — domestic, clerical, service and retail work — where they have low-paid and low-status jobs

- job segregation like this results from outdated and often inefficient employment practices, and positive action can help to create opportunities for women

- positive action can help women to acquire the skills required to enter a wider range of jobs, can maximise the potential of women employees, and is necessary to encourage women to contribute fully to the organisation where they work, including returning to their jobs after raising children, and seeking promotion

AFFIRMATIVE ACTION

In Northern Ireland, the main anti-discrimination legislation is concerned with ensuring fair participation in the workforce by Catholics and Protestants and by people of different political persuasions. A slightly different legal terminology is used, and they have a different system called *Affirmative Action*.

Affirmative action is a key feature of the Fair Employment Act. It has two main features:

> 1. *It requires both the adoption of practices encouraging fair participation and the changing or stopping of practices that restrict or discourage such participation.*
> 2. *It requires forward thinking to identify potential problems and the adoption of remedial measures.*

You must set goals and a timetable for the achievement of these goals as part of affirmative action. This can be done by employers or it might be specified by the Commission if it thinks they are necessary.

> **Case law**
> Magill v. Barney 1993. The Fair Employment Tribunal has found that there was less favourable treatment of a Roman Catholic employee, subjected to the display of sectarian graffiti and singing and whistling of 'Orange' marching tunes. The tribunal was satisfied that if the employees had been singing pro-republican songs the management would have taken action.

QUOTAS FOR PEOPLE WITH DISABILITIES

If your organisation has more than 20 people working in it, then 3% of the employees should be registered disabled people. If you currently do not fill this quota, then every vacancy should be offered to a registered disabled person. If there isn't such a person available to do the job, then the employer can get a permit to employ a non-disabled person.

It is not an offence to be below the quota, but it is an offence to be below quota and to employ a person who is not registered disabled without getting a permit to do so.

People tend to underestimate the potential of disabled people. In fact, most jobs can be carried out by someone with a disability, although some adaptation may be necessary on behalf of the organisation (for example to the building or office space). In addition, many aids and grants are available through government schemes to help employers employ or retain people with disabilities — see Chapter 5.

The government 'double tick' logo, 'POSITIVE ABOUT DISABLED PEOPLE', can be used in an advertisement as long as you have measures in place to be welcoming and fair to people with disabilities. Since June 1993 the Employment Department has asked any organisation that uses the symbol to make a public pledge to substantiate its commitment through practical measures. The commitment is to:

- offer a guaranteed interview to all applicants with a disability who meet the minimum criteria for an advertised post

- consult employees with disabilities at least once a year about what can be done to make sure they can develop and use their abilities at work

- make every effort to keep employees in employment if they become disabled

- take action to ensure that key employees develop an awareness of the needs of people with disabilities so that their commitments can be effective

- review the commitment annually — consider achievements, plan improvements and inform all employees about progress and future plans

To help employers with this initiative, the Employment Department has set up local Placing, Assessing and Counselling Teams (PACTs) around the country. These bring together the work previously done by the Disablement Advisory Service and the Employment Rehabilitation Service. For details of your local PACT, contact the Employment Department.

GENUINE OCCUPATIONAL QUALIFICATION

Both the Race Relations Act and the Sex Discrimination Act have sections that cover the situations when you are specifically allowed to advertise for a woman or for man or for a person from a particular racial group. Any such exemptions must be quoted in the text of the advertisement.

- the Race Relations Act (section 5(2)(d)) permits the selection of people on racial grounds for a job where they will provide those of their own racial group with 'personal services promoting their welfare, and those services can most effectively be provided by someone of that racial group'

- the sex Discrimination Act (section 7(2)(e)) allows the recruitment of specifically women or men to a particular post.

See Chapter 7 for more details of both Genuine Occupational Qualification rules.

REMOVING BARRIERS

Other aspects of the recruitment process can create obvious or more subtle barriers for people in different sections of the community, which may result in discrimination. These types of discrimination, although not technically unlawful, should also be removed. For example:

AGE

- don't insist on an age requirement
- don't put age ranges in the job advert, or expect ages on a CV

HIV AND AIDS

- don't ask for a blood test automatically
- make sure your health and safety standards are up to scratch

PEOPLE WITH DISABILITIES

- use the √√ symbol
- make an effort in job adverts to encourage applications from people with disabilities

- find out about their disability and welcome them to interview accordingly
- don't use medical checks as a barrier to competence

ACTION SUMMARY

Use Positive Action measures to meet your equality targets:

- provide training for those not already in employment
- provide training for those in employment
- consider whether it is appropriate to encourage people to apply to jobs where they have been underrepresented over the past 12 months
- encourage job applications in the interests of fair participation (Northern Ireland)
- use the wording of the advert to encourage underrepresented groups to apply (men, women, racial groups, registered people with disabilities)
- use the quota system for people with disabilities
- decide if you need a Genuine Occupational Qualification exemption for any post being advertised

But remember, Don't

- discriminate against employees with HIV or AIDS
- set age barriers
- deliberately discriminate against any group of people

1.3 MONITORING

It is essential to monitor your equality management; otherwise, how do you know:

- the nature and extent of the inequalities that exist at present in the organisation?
- if you are achieving the targets you have set yourself?

An integral part of your overall equality management strategy is to monitor two things:

- **The composition of the existing workforce**
  Once you have seen where the inequalities lie, you can plan your strategy and set targets, then implement detailed policies and procedures to redress any direct or indirect discrimination.
  After that you can take regular snapshots of the organisation to see trends in making equality work.

- **Recruitment, selection, appointment and promotion decisions.**

The information recorded from both exercises has four main uses:

- to provide statistics related to your targets
- to be used in the case of a grievance
- to improve the recruitment and selection procedure
- to improve management decision-making

Although the employer should take the first steps, staff at all levels of the organisation should be consulted through the trade union or other recognised channels before the policy is made final. This is particularly important where record keeping is to be introduced.

Employers holding information on computer about employees' ethnic origins or other personal profiles must be registered under the Data Protection Act, and are obliged to be accurate and give subjects access to the information. Specified detailed guidance on keeping details of ethnic origin is available from the Data Protection Registrar. See Chapter 7 for more details.

The legislation affecting employers in Northern Ireland is very strict about monitoring and is very specific about what information has to be recorded and how long it has to be kept for. See Chapter 7 and contact the Fair Employment Commission for an information pack.

WHAT TO MONITOR

MONITORING PEOPLE OF DIFFERENT ETHNIC ORIGINS

The purpose of keeping ethnic records is not a social survey, but to see whether some people are being treated less favourably than others on grounds of race, colour or ethnic origin.

The CRE recommends that the following classification system is used in ethnic monitoring:

>White
>Black: Caribbean
>Black: African
>Black: Other (please specify)
>Indian
>Pakistani
>Bangladeshi
>Chinese
>Other (please specify)

Classification by place of birth is inadequate as an indicator, because birthplace does not correspond to race or colour. Classification by black and white alone does not make sufficient distinction between the different groups.

Classification by a combination of colour and ethnic origin is recommended by the CRE because it enables those people born in the UK, but whose origins are not white European, to fill in the questionnaire in such a way as to stress their colour and origins without any suggestion that they 'belong' elsewhere.

MONITORING WOMEN

It is important to monitor where women are in the organisation and their progress within it, their levels of seniority, applications for training, regrading and promotion, records of job applicants and appointments.

MONITORING PEOPLE WITH DISABILITIES

As has been made clear, people with disabilities face discrimination both in access to employment and in employment. Monitor as above to record the success of the equal opportunities policy, and to check whether the organisation has achieved the quota required.

MONITORING RELIGION (IN NORTHERN IRELAND)

Monitoring is a valuable tool in determining whether or not members of the Protestant or Catholic communities are enjoying or are likely to enjoy fair participation in the workforce. The ideal is to identify any job category within the workforce for which there are fewer applicants or workers of a particular community background than might be expected. Employers have to complete an annual monitoring return to the FEC.

MONITORING AGE

The Institute of Personnel Management recommendations on age discrimination include monitoring your workforce at intervals to find out whether or not there is any indication of unfair discrimination against particular age groups.

MONITORING LESBIANS AND GAY MEN

Include lesbians and gay men in any monitoring exercise. If you include a question on a self-monitoring form, then people can chose to fill it in or not. As long as the process remains confidential, then lesbians and gay men can be assured the privacy and security they need at work. If the reasons for monitoring are explained thoroughly to job applicants and workers, the information can be gained without fear that it will be used to increase discrimination rather than to prevent it. This fear is borne out by the recent survey by Stonewall found that 48% of lesbian and gay respondents to a questionnaire on employment had been harassed at work because of their sexuality.

HOW TO MONITOR

THE CURRENT WORKFORCE

Records on the current workforce and trainees will identify where groups are in the workforce and their progress in relation to other groups of colleagues.

Set aside a particular day or week to survey the existing workers. The survey should be publicised beforehand and explained and negotiated with the trade unions or employee representatives before it is carried out, so that people fully understand the nature and reasons for the survey.

APPLICATION FORMS

The model of recruitment followed in this handbook is to use application forms, and not CVs or unsolicited letters, in order to get standard information on applicants and for monitoring purposes (see Chapter 2).

A monitoring form should be included in the package of materials sent out to candidates. If possible, include an envelope in the package so that applicants can return the form under separate cover and hence the monitoring remains separate from the application. If this is not economically viable, then candidates could be invited to return the form separately if they wish. This is important in giving applicants confidence that the monitoring is not going to be used against them in their application. It is vital to explain the use to which the monitoring forms will be put, who will have access to them and the confidentiality of the forms.

For Example:
We aim to be an equal opportunity employer and select staff solely on merit irrespective of race, sex, disability, sexuality, etc. In order to monitor the effectiveness of our equal opportunity policy we request all applicants to provide the information requested. This will be kept confidential to the selection panel and will be seen by them only after the recruitment process has been completed.

Two methods of monitoring can be used:

1. The monitoring form is not numbered and there is no way of tying the information on the form to the application, unless the candidate returns the two in the same envelope. With this method you can monitor the profile of applicants and you can get the details of the

EQUALITY TARGETS AND MONITORING

successful appointee, but you can not monitor the shortlisting process.

2. The monitoring form and application form are numbered so that the forms can be tied in with the applications after the shortlisting process. The form is still returned in a separate envelope and is kept separate until after the recruitment has finished. It is possible to monitor the profile of applicants, shortlisting and final appointment.

In the latter case it is particularly important to explain the purpose of the numbers and how the form will be used during the recruitment process. An example of a monitoring form using the second approach appears below.

Sample equal opportunities monitoring form

Application Number_____

We would be grateful if you would fill in this form and return it with your application. We are working towards equal opportunities and this information will help us to monitor our advertising, selection and appointment systems.

The information will not be used as part of the selection process itself and is held, confidential and anonymous, separately from the application forms until after the appointment has been made.

1 Are you MALE/FEMALE?

2 What is your sexuality?

3 Do you have a disability? YES/NO

(Continued overleaf)

> **Sample equal opportunities monitoring form (contd)**
>
> 4 How old are you?
> Under 25 25–39 40–54 55–65 65 +
>
> 5 How would you describe your ethnic origin? [CRE sample list]
>
> White   _____
>
> Black: African   _____
>
> Black: Caribbean   _____
>
> Black: Other (please specify) _____
>
> Indian   _____
>
> Pakistani   _____
>
> Bangladeshi   _____
>
> Chinese   _____
>
> Other (please specify)   _____
>
> 5 Post applied for?
>
> 6 Where did you see this job advertised?

SELECTION AND APPOINTMENT

The next step is to monitor the profile of those shortlisted and the appointee. This will indicate if any direct or indirect discrimination is occurring in the selection process. If, for example, women represent 50% of the shortlist but only 10% of those appointed for a range of jobs, then you might suspect some form of discrimination. Keep records of interviews, and appointments for 12 months. [3 yrs in Northern Ireland]

PROMOTION AND TRAINING

Collect information about promotions and access to training courses for those eligible, those shortlisted and those selected.

> **Case law**
> Richards v. Brighton Borough Council. An Afro-Caribbean woman with over 13 years' relevant experience who was passed over for a job in preference for a white woman graduate with little relevant experience was discriminated against on the grounds of race. The failure to make notes on the selection process and the failure to introduce monitoring of the equal opportunity policy were taken into account.

ANALYSIS

Once you have all the information, you will be able to work out the proportion of various groups in the workforce at various levels. This can be compared with the proportion of the groups nationally or in the local area and will show whether there is any underrepresentation or concentration in any particular types of work, grades or levels, departments or location.

You will also be able to see if any groups have a greater or lower success rate or access rate than others in selection, promotion and access to training.

ACTION SUMMARY

- plan the monitoring process properly
- consult with staff reps and trade unions representatives
- keep the results confidential

- analyse the results
- use the results to take further action

1.4 ACTION SUMMARY

- draw up a clear policy to promote equal opportunities throughout your work and management practices
- ensure that the overall responsibility for policies and practices relating to equal opportunities is allocated to a senior manager
- appoint an equality manager to oversee the management of the programme
- develop clear targets and performance indicators relating to equal opportunities management
- ensure that policies and practices are communicated clearly to existing employees, new recruits, job applicants and potential applicants
- provide training for staff in key decision-making areas, e.g. senior executives, personnel staff, managerial staff, recruiters and selectors, supervisory staff and reception area staff
- consult with appropriate recognised trade unions, employee representatives or the workforce on the implementation of equal opportunities policies and any amendments to practices
- make it clear that breaches of equal opportunities practice constitute misconduct and that disciplinary proceedings may result

- include positive action, affirmative action, goals, targets and timetables as part of any equal opportunities policy

1.5 LEGAL SUMMARY

- **Equality targets** are further explained and laid out in the CRE and EOC Codes of Practice

- **Positive action** measures are described in the **Race Relations Act 1976,** sections 37, 38, and the **Sex Discrimination Act 1975,** sections 47, 48

- **Affirmative action** for those working in Northern Ireland comes under the **Fair Employment (NI) Act 1989**

- **Quotas** for people with disabilities are covered in the **Disabled Persons Employment Act**

- **Genuine Occupational Qualification** can be found in the **Race Relations Act 1976,** section 5 and the **Sex Discrimination Act 1975,** section 7

- **Monitoring** is covered in the FEA, CRE and EOC Codes of Practice, and the CRE has produced several books and booklets on the topic

- **Keeping information on computer** is regulated by the **Data Protection Act 1984,** and guidance is issued by the Data Protection Registrar

2 RECRUITMENT

Formal and standard recruitment methods lie at the heart of a good equal opportunities management system. Setting up procedures and sticking to them will produce the best results.

If you view your recruits as people with potential rather than as men and women, black and white, then you will recruit the best person for the job free from prejudiced notions. Getting to this stage is difficult, however, because we tend to make snap judgements based on what we see. Careful preparation for interviews and monitoring of the results help to overcome this tendency.

KEY CONCEPTS

- exit interview
- vacancy analysis
- person specification
- job definition
- application form

QUESTIONS ANSWERED

- how do I conduct an exit interview?
- how do I collect information for a job description?
- do I always have to advertise jobs?
- how do I write a person specification that works?
- should application forms always have the same questions on them?
- what are the most effective recruitment methods?

CONTENTS

1: ***Vacancy analysis***
   Information collection
       Job analysis
       Exit interviews
   Flexible ways of working
   Action summary

2: ***The recruitment process***
   Responsibility for co-ordination and consultation
   The job description
       The needs of the organisation
       Review positive action measures
       Writing a good job description
   The person specification
       How to write the person specification
   Criteria selection
   Recruitment methods
       Attracting people with disabilities
   Advertising
       Where to advertise
       The content of the advert
   The design of key documents
       Covering letter
       The application form
       Equal opportunities policy
       Equal opportunities monitoring form
       General job information, including terms and conditions
   Administration
   Action summary

3: ***Action summary***

4: ***Legal summary***

2.1 VACANCY ANALYSIS

When a vacancy arises or new work becomes available in your organisation, this is a good opportunity for you to assess the best and most cost-effective way to get the work done that incorporates equal opportunities. The question answered in this section is: 'Do I need to recruit or can I get it done in other ways?'

The process used to decide this is:

1. collect information from job analysis and exit interviews;
2. define how flexible you can be about getting the work done;
3. decide whether to recruit or not.

INFORMATION COLLECTION

JOB ANALYSIS

Job analysis is the process of *collecting and analysing* information about the tasks, responsibilities, performance standards, working conditions and working relationships of jobs. The information to be collected varies to some extent with the purpose of the analysis, but the usual categories of basic information are:

- **Job identification data:** job title, department, division, organisation name, location.

- **Relationships with others:** reporting relationships, supervisory relationships, liaison within the organisation, external contacts and liaison, co-ordinating relationships.

- **Job content:** actual tasks or duties of the job, level of responsibility for tasks, importance of tasks, how often performed.
- **Working conditions:** physical environment; social environment, such as working alone or in a group, usual time of work; economic environment, such as salary and benefits.
- **Performance standards or objectives:** these can either be for the job as a whole or for specific tasks, and can be expressed in quantitative terms (such as, raising £x per annum) or in qualitative terms (such as, maintaining group cohesiveness).

So the end-result of job analysis will be:

- job description
- person specification
- performance standards for use in staff supervision and appraisal, discipline and grievance procedures, monitoring and evaluation
- reporting relationships for accountability
- contacts and liaison relationships internal and external to the organisation
- working conditions particular to the post

EXIT INTERVIEWS

The purpose of an exit interview with an outgoing worker is to find out their reasons for leaving and if there are any implications for the future management of the post or the organisation. They might have useful information for the future design of the job, the job description and the person specifications.

Some employees might find this an intimidating experience and may not respond well. Interviewers will need to listen rather than question and be low key rather than intimidating.

The interview should cover the following points:

- reasons for leaving
- training needs — were they met?
- structure of the organisation, if appropriate
- working relationships and support available
- management issues
- salary
- job satisfaction, effectiveness, etc.
- changes in the job specification

FLEXIBLE WAYS OF WORKING

When a post becomes vacant or a new post is created this is a great opportunity to look at introducing more flexible working arrangements. You could perhaps introduce:

- part-time working
- job sharing
- term-time working
- working from home
- flexible working
- fixed-term working

The most obvious way of filling a vacancy is to recruit a new worker to carry out the job in a similar way to the current postholder, but it is worth considering if the post could be filled in some other way. Some alternatives to recruiting a new worker are:

- reorganise the work
- use overtime (this has to be managed to make sure it is healthy and cost effective)
- make the job part-time
- subcontract the work
- use an agency to provide temporary personnel

All flexible working options are of special interest to single parents, people with disabilities and people with caring responsibilities. There is more information in Chapter 6.

Job reorganisation in particular could help the employment of people with disabilities, where they can do most of a job but not one part of it.

Looking at these alternatives will provide you with enough information to decide whether to proceed with an external recruitment process. Even if you do not need a new worker, you will need a new job description and person specification to help you to decide which of the current workers you will ask to fill the gap.

ACTION SUMMARY

- gather the information needed to write the job description and person specification
- decide if it is suitable to offer flexitime or job sharing on the post or other flexible working deals

- decide whether to reallocate the work within existing workforce or whether to recruit new staff

Do

- take the time to plan and think about each vacancy
- describe accurately the requirements and duties of the job

But remember, Don't

- just fill the job again without carrying out a review
- ignore opportunities to introduce flexible working

2.2 THE RECRUITMENT PROCESS

RESPONSIBILITY FOR CO-ORDINATION AND CONSULTATION

If you have decided that you need more personnel as a result of vacancy analysis, then you need to start the recruitment process as soon as possible. It is a complex process and the more systematic and well organised you are the better. It makes sense to consult widely to begin with and then to spend time drawing up the job definition and person specification, as this will save a lot of work later on.

As a line manager you may or may not have to do all of this yourself. This section is a guide to the personnel process, even if you are not directly involved in it.

The sample consultation and responsibility chart on p. 39 assumes that the post is advertised.

Sample consultation and responsibility chart

Event or task	Responsibility	Timetable (Line manager to complete)
1. Notice of intention to resign	Current postholder	
2. Exit interview held Vacancy analysis carried out New post agreed + funded	Line manager Personnel Dept/ Senior management	
3. Job definition procedures followed, grading decided if necessary	Line management/ Personnel	
4. Recruitment process and dates agreed; selection panel set up	Senior management/ Personnel/ Line manager	
5. Job description, person specification, advert, background	Line manager	

(Continued overleaf)

Sample consultation and responsibility chart (Contd)

information all drafted, take decision on positive action measures, consult personnel dept

6. Job description, person specification, advert content and placement, background information all agreed — Line manager

  Line manager

7. Advert sent to press — Support staff

8. Advert appears

9. Job description, background information, application form, equal opportunities statement, details of premises, monitoring form sent to enquirers — Support staff

(Continued overleaf)

> **Sample consultation and responsibility chart (contd)**
>
> 10. Completed application forms returned
>
> 11. Monitoring forms detached   Support staff
>
> 12. Closing date   2/3 weeks after point 8

THE JOB DESCRIPTION

Not many organisations feel they can spare the time to carry out a full job analysis each time they write a job description. However, it can ensure the future success of the job. A clear job description provides a sound basis for:

Individual:	recruitment and selection
	staff appraisal
	staff supervision
	induction
	staff development
	discipline and grievance procedures
Organisational:	restructuring and review
	training needs analysis
	staff/team relations
Industrial relations:	job evaluation

Once each job description in the team is right, many other management processes and practices fall into place.

THE NEEDS OF THE ORGANISATION

Job descriptions **MUST BE BASED ON THE NEEDS OF THE ORGANISATION AND ITS CORE PURPOSE OR SERVICE DELIVERY STANDARDS**, not on the needs or personal preferences of the individual currently performing the task.

If boundaries are clearly set and standards are properly determined, monitored and evaluated, all workers can benefit from:

- a clear understanding of the purpose of their job
- a clear understanding of its importance to the organisation and its relation to other jobs in their team
- better supervision
- monitoring and evaluation that are firmly based and less threatening
- less worker stress
- less risk of disputes that are costly in time and money

Avoiding mistakes

Many job descriptions come about through:

- organic development of what the manager or senior management think needs doing
- what the previous job holder was good at and saw as important
- a conglomeration of what the outgoing job holder and other people don't want to do
- developing from what a volunteer was doing (in voluntary organisations)

- being copied from another organisation
- a generic collective duties description
- what seemed like a good idea at the time

All of these sources have their problems!
Lack of clarity in a job description may lead to:

- confusion for individuals that might result in discipline and grievance problems (at worst, an industrial tribunal)
- a lack of clear direction for the organisation
- team problems over different interpretations of job descriptions or of the importance of the various tasks within the job description

Therefore DON'T:

- just use the same old job description for the next job unless you're sure it is still right for the job
- create a job description out of the bits of work no one else wants to do — this will create an impossible job that will have a high staff turnover and/or high staff stress level, either of which will be costly in terms of management time, staff time and general unhappiness at work
- mix radically different skill areas in one job description — such as finance and fundraising, personnel and computer manager. The following combinations are more possible, but you could consider part-time workers for the different discrete skill areas instead.

    Finance and Administration
    Fundraising and Public Relations
    Office and Computer manager

Membership and Personnel management
Training and Development
Advice and Information

REVIEW POSITIVE ACTION MEASURES

The equality targets and positive action measures outlined in Chapter 1 should be reviewed and a decision taken on which ones are appropriate to use. These should be incorporated in the person specification or advert or both.

For example:

'All applicants with disabilities who meet the selection criteria will be guaranteed an interview.'

'Person from the African Caribbean community is required. Genuine Occupational Qualification RRA Section 5(2)(d) applies.'

'We particularly welcome applications from suitably qualified women as women have been underrepresented in this work over the last 12 months.'

'This factory has an equal opportunities policy. Management proposes to run a special course for female operatives who wish to become qualified for promotion to inspector grade.'

WRITING A GOOD JOB DESCRIPTION

Gathering all the necessary information to write a clear job description can be a difficult task.

First you must be clear about:

- the aim and purpose of the job
- the tasks that need doing
- the relationship to other jobs in the organisation

- how it fits in with the organisation's priorities
- what sort of support the job gets or gives to other staff

Sources of information

These vary, depending on whether you are writing a new job description or reviewing an old one.

For a job description for a NEW JOB:

- the needs of the service
- the priorities of the organisation
- monitoring and evaluation information
- interviews with colleagues
- similar posts in other organisations

For a job description for an EXISTING JOB:

- *existing written information*
  Is it up to date?
  Is it accurate?
  Is it detailed enough?
  Is it consistent?
  Does it provide the information in the way you would wish?

- *interview with the postholder/colleagues/line manager*
  Interviews are time consuming and need to be carried out on the basis of a coherent plan.
      The job holder has the most detailed knowledge of the job being done and is obviously a key source of information, but this information may be biased. If the information is from an exit interview with a person who is leaving, their view of the organisation may influence their judgement.

The manager may want to change the role anyway.

If there is no one in post, then colleagues may be a useful source in addition to the postholder's line manager.

- *consultation with personnel department, senior managers.*

THE PERSON SPECIFICATION

Every job must have a person specification, as it provides the basis for:

- the advertisement
- the application form
- shortlisting
- interview questions
- the final decision between candidates

The person specification should list the essential characteristics needed to carry out the job. These might include:

- experience
- knowledge
- skills and abilities
- qualifications
- education/training
- other requirements, e.g. to travel, to drive
- legal requirements

The criteria should be as specific as possible without being intimidating. All selection criteria must be carefully established before recruitment is put in motion. Factors other than formal qualifications and work experience (for example, skills and transferable life experience) may be used.

Every candidate shortlisted should meet all the essential criteria. If no candidate meets all essential criteria, you may need to re-advertise rather than change the rules half way through the recruitment process. (See the section on shortlisting in Chapter 3.)

HOW TO WRITE THE PERSON SPECIFICATION

1. Go through the job description and write a list of all the criteria you think are necessary. Every requirement should match tasks from the job description.

2. Make a distinction between essential and desirable requirements (see sample person specification on p. 50):

    - **essential criteria** are the basic level that must be met or exceeded if the task is to be performed adequately or successfully.

    - **desirable criteria** function only to help the panel to decide whom to shortlist if there are a large number of candidates meeting all the essential criteria, and whom to employ if there is a tie between candidates.

    Don't set unnecessarily high standards where physical ability is concerned, as you may exclude people with disabilities. Unnecessary factors that might prevent some people from applying are: stamina, good eyesight, acute hearing, physical strength and mobility.

Don't set unnecessarily high education standards or specify English qualifications only (this constitutes indirect racial discrimination).

Don't use age or age-related criteria unless this factor has been clearly identified as a positive action measure to attract more individuals from underrepresented age groups.

The CRE Code of Practice recommends that overseas degrees, diplomas and other qualifications that are comparable with UK qualifications should be accepted as equivalents.

3. Distinguish between appointment by potential or attainment when constructing essential criteria:

- *attainment*: candidates already have the skills

- *potential*: candidates have the potential to learn

    This distinction is crucial because sometimes the requirements could come only from working experience, in which case the category would come under attainment.

    If potential is decided on, then words like 'ability to . . .' rather than 'experience of . . .' can be used in drawing up the criteria.

    It may be more difficult to test if candidates have the potential to do something rather than the ability to do it. This needs careful thought before deciding between using potential and attainment.

4. Ensure that each requirement can be measured or tested in some way.

Define the essential elements of the skill or ability and then devise questions to elicit that information on the application form or at interview. Alternatively, use selection tests.

For example:
If the criterion is 'potential ability to manage', decide what constitutes an ability to manage. Let's say you decide on:

Supervision skills
Decision-making and prioritising skills
Planning skills
Teamwork skills
Leadership skills

You then devise questions to test (a) their theoretical knowledge and (b) their existing skills. You could also use some kind of group test, such as decision-making or group prioritising or negotiation.

SUMMARY

Make your draft list of criteria. Go back and check:

- do they match a job description requirement?
- are they non-discriminatory?
- are they testable or measurable in some way?
- do they overlap with any other criterion? Can you amalgamate one or two?

Any criterion that passes the above questions can be added to the person specification.

Sample person specification

JOB TITLE: Finance Assistant

CRITERIA	ESSENTIAL	DESIRABLE
1. SKILLS AND ABILITIES	Numeracy Attention to detail Accuracy of work Ability to work on own initiative	
2. EXPERIENCE	2 yrs financial administration Processing invoices writing financial reports	computerised PAYE system specific Accounts software eg BONUS
3. KNOWLEDGE	Equal Opportunities Policy	Pension schemes
4. EDUCATION/ TRAINING	GCSE Maths or equivalent	
5. GENERAL REQUIREMENTS	Ability to work in a team willing to accept and use supervision.	

ACTION SUMMARY

- set the recruitment process in motion
- draft a timetable
- liaise with the personnel department
- review any positive action measures or equality targets set

- include them in the person specification or adverts as necessary
- follow the procedure for writing job descriptions
- follow the procedure for writing person specifications

Do

- be well organised and systematic
- consult widely, including on equal opportunities targets
- consider the needs of the organisation first and foremost — not the needs of individual workers or teams
- write a clear job description
- produce a specification of the essential/desirable aptitudes and characteristics of the person required to carry out the job satisfactorily

But remember, Don't

- use the old job description without checking
- mix radically different skill areas in one job description
- specify skills or qualities that are too general or not measurable

RECRUITMENT METHODS

The following are the most common methods of recruitment, listed in order of their use by personnel professionals.

Adverts in regional press	87%
Adverts in specialist press	80%
Adverts in national press	78%
Job centres	71%
Employment agencies	62%
Recruitment consultants	61%
Executive search consultants	36%
Careers fairs	35%
Open days	32%
University milk rounds	21%
Radio advertising	17%

Advertising is the method most widely used and will be dealt with in most depth here. Although adverts can be costly, they will bring in a wider range of people.

It is not advisable to use recruitment consultants or executive search consultants (head hunters) as they may rely on word of mouth or on people they know personally to recommend for a particular job.

Careers fairs, open days and university milk rounds all have a special place in recruitment and can be a good way to target applicants from particularly underrepresented sectors in your workforce.

In general, as long as the method has a wide circulation and will attract people outside of current employment, then you are being fair and non-discriminatory.

Example:
Sainsbury's in Bolton was able to fill 40 out of 300 vacancies with members of ethnic minority groups by working with Bolton Racial Equality Council to increase the flow of black applicants.

Whichever method you use, all the recruitment and advertising documentation will still need to conform to equal opportunities standards.

ATTRACTING PEOPLE WITH DISABILITIES

- advertise in the usual way and encourage people with disabilities to apply either by using the √√ symbol or by including the wording 'We welcome applications from people with disabilities'

- advertise in specialist press, local disability newsletters, and through leaflets to local disability organisations

- contact specialist organisations and networks that exist to assist employers and individual job-seekers:
  - Disablement Resettlement Officers at the local job centre and staff at Employment Rehabilitation Centres could help in recruiting people with disabilities;
  - specialist careers officers or special schools may be able to help in putting employers in touch with younger people or school leavers.

ADVERTISING

It is the role of the manager to ensure that the advertisement is accurate and sent off in time to meet the deadlines — although another employee may actually carry out the task.

WHERE TO ADVERTISE

A choice should be made between:

- *a local trawl* — suitable where a good range of applicants will be available locally, e.g. for administrative, lower-level finance posts. These posts are unlikely to be 'different' enough to encourage mobility from outside the local area.

- *a national trawl* — suitable where the numbers and quality of applicants may be limited by making a local restriction, and/or where the attraction of the job will mean quality candidates will be prepared to be mobile.

The following are broad guidelines for where to advertise. If you're taking positive action or affirmative action measures, then place the advert in the press read by the underrepresented community.

Local: local/regional press
job centre, including Disablement Resettlement Officer
local black press where available
specialist local disability organisations

National: national press
national ethnic minority press
appropriate trade/professional press, e.g. *Personnel Management* for personnel managers
Scottish press for jobs in Scotland
Northern Ireland press
specialist disability press

Costs must always be taken into account, which will mean restricting the trawl in some instances. This is likely to be particularly the case with temporary or part-time posts.

THE CONTENT OF THE ADVERT

The following must be in the advert:

- the organisation's name and logo
- the job title
- where the job is based
- a general idea of the duties involved and any qualifications required
- the salary (either the amount or the scale if you use a recognised one), and any allowances
- the equal opportunities statement (brief version)
- the job sharer's statement (if you have a policy on job sharing)
- the closing date
- where to get further details — include a phone number

Include the following if they are applicable:

- the duration of the post if it is for a fixed term
- the hours if it is not full time
- a statement of any positive action, encouragement to apply
- a reference to any Genuine Occupational Qualification exemptions you are using under the Race Relations or Sex Discrimination Acts
- the double tick √√ symbol used by the Department of Employment to symbolise commitment to good practice in the employment

of people with disabilities (see the positive action section in Chapter 1).

When a post does not require previous experience or where training can be given, then state this.

THE DESIGN OF KEY DOCUMENTS

COVERING LETTER

The covering letter to enquirers should:

- remind applicants of the closing date
- state the interview dates if known
- tell applicants if receipt of their form will be automatically acknowledged or not
- point out the monitoring form and give full reasons why it is included
- inform people when they can expect to hear if they are shortlisted, and whether they will be told if they are not shortlisted.
- include details of when you would like people to start if there are any particular considerations.

There is a sample covering letter on p. 57.

Sample covering letter

Date

Dear Enquirer,

JOB TITLE

Thank you for your enquiry about this post.

Please find enclosed:

- A job description and person specification
- An application form
- General information about the job and the organisation
- The equal opportunities policy
- An equal opportunities monitoring form (please return this with your application form; this information is for monitoring purposes only and will not be used as part of the selection procedure)

Applicants will be shortlisted according to how well they meet the criteria in the person specification. Please highlight and explain how you meet these using the application form. Please do not include a CV.

All application forms will be acknowledged and you will be informed by post whether you have been shortlisted or not.

Interviews will take place in . . . on . . .

We look forward to receiving your application by . . . at the latest.

Yours sincerely,

Manager

THE APPLICATION FORM

The purpose of the application form is to see if people meet the criteria on the person specification. Therefore it must ask specific questions based on those criteria. Each application form will need different specific questions as well as some standard features. There is a sample application form at the end of the chapter (pp. 65–69).

The form should be easy to fill in, have enough space for clear answers and provide the information needed for shortlisting.

The form should be designed using the following points:

Personal details You need only ask for name, address and phone number. For equal opportunities purposes, these could be on a front sheet that could be detached from the main body of the form after both have been numbered. This adds to anonymity in shortlisting.

Access needs Ask a question on applicants' access or other needs in order to be able to attend the interview.

Past criminal offences Questions about criminal convictions should not be asked as a matter of course, but included only when absolutely necessary, following the criteria in the Rehabilitation of Offenders Act.

For certain jobs it is essential to ask about previous criminal convictions — for example, for all jobs in places required to register under the Registered Homes Act and those providing young people under 18 with accommodation, care, social services or training. For a full list of occupations exempt under the Act, consult the Home Office or an up-to-date employment law manual. See Chapter 7 for a fuller exposition of the law.

References Ask for two referees and ask if they can be contacted before interview or only if you are to offer them the post. See Chapter 4 for a more detailed discussion of references.

Main part of the form The main part of the form should have questions relating to the skills, experience and abilities needed for the job. Each point in the person specification should be covered, and there should be a specific question related to each point.

- do not include irrelevant questions — for example, asking for all educational qualifications since 'O' levels, when experience gained in other ways is more important.

- make questions as specifically related to the post as possible. For instance, if recruiting an advice worker, you might ask on equal opportunities:

    What do you think are the key issues in implementing an equal opportunities policy in a neighbourhood advice centre?

- ask about people's ability to travel, possession of a driving licence, etc., if this is relevant, but do not ask things like whether they have dependants, and then assume, if they have, that they cannot work unsocial hours. This could lead to discrimination against people with dependants and people with disabilities. Instead, ask simply if they are prepared to work unsocial hours. It will be possible to make clear in the interview what the hours of work are and to ask if they have understood this and can work at those times.

Layout The layout of the form is important. The form should be 4–5 sides long with adequate space for each answer, as this gives the applicants a good idea of the importance you attach to each question and the amount you want them to write.

EQUAL OPPORTUNITIES POLICY

The equal opportunity statement and policy should always be included.

EQUAL OPPORTUNITIES MONITORING FORM

The monitoring form should be sent to all candidates, with a full explanation in the covering letter and on the form itself of why you are carrying out monitoring. (See the sample form in Chapter 1.)

GENERAL JOB INFORMATION, INCLUDING TERMS AND CONDITIONS

The following information should be included in a separate document:

- how the job fits into the project and organisation
- details of any induction, supervision, support
- details of career opportunities and training available in the job
- the amount of travelling and overnight stays involved and whether caring costs are paid in those circumstances
- the accessibility of the office
- whether the job is open to job sharers, and under what terms and conditions they would be employed
- terms and conditions:
  Remind applicants of the salary and scale. Include any attractive terms and conditions in the contract: e.g. holiday entitlement, job-sharing or flexible

working scheme, better than statutory maternity leave, pension arrangements, relocation terms, etc.

ADMINISTRATION

A key aspect of successful recruitment is the administration process. Brief your support staff or administration team on the following issues.

RESPONDING TO ENQUIRIES

Receptionists or people handling enquiries over the phone need to be well briefed on equal opportunities matters. They should never take it upon themselves to discourage any potential applicant from applying.

They should be welcoming and make sure they get the name and address of the caller accurately. If applicants want more information about the details of the job before being sent the job package, they can be asked to wait until they have received this. If they want substantive information after receiving the jobs package, they should always be passed on to a member of the selection team.

> **Case law**
> Chave v. Kandy Toys Distributors 1992. Ms Chave telephoned Kandy Toys to enquire about a job advertised in the warehouse involving the manual loading of products onto lorries for distribution. She was told that the company would not take on women for the job because it involved heavy lifting. The tribunal found in her favour when she complained of unlawful sex discrimination.

Information should always be sent out within 24 hours of receiving an enquiry, as a matter of courtesy and to maintain efficiency.

RECEIVING APPLICATION AND MONITORING FORMS

All application forms and any material sent with them must be carefully kept together. The personnel opening envelopes should paperclip or staple as necessary, taking care to detach the monitoring form (after numbering).

When the application forms are returned, the front and second sheets of the application form and the equal opportunities monitoring form should all be numbered with the same number. The administrator needs to keep a list of consecutive numbers with the tray where the forms are to be kept. These must be crossed off in order of use.

Each of the three items — the front page, the rest of the application form, the equal opportunities monitoring form — should be placed in separate trays and kept confidential. The main part of the application form should be confidential to the selection panel, and the rest of the documentation should be kept confidential until after the completion of the selection process. A named person should be delegated to look after applications for each post; these must be kept for monitoring purposes.

All application forms should be acknowledged, if financial and administrative resources permit.

ACTION SUMMARY

- set the recruitment process in motion
- draft a timetable
- liaise with the personnel department
- review any positive action measures or equality targets set

- include them in the person specification or adverts as necessary
- follow the procedure for writing job descriptions
- follow the procedure for writing person specifications

Do

- be well organised and systematic
- consult widely, including on equal opportunities targets
- consider the needs of the organisation first and foremost — not the needs of individual workers or teams
- review any positive action measures or equality targets set
- include them in the person specification or adverts as necessary
- write a clear job description
- produce a specification of the essential/desirable aptitudes and characteristics of the person required to carry out the job satisfactorily

But remember, Don't

- use the old job description without checking
- mix radically different skill areas in one job description
- specify skills or qualities that are too general or not measurable

Sample Standard Application Form

This sample form demonstrates the design features of application forms.

    Page 1   standard except for the job title
    Page 2   standard
    Pages 3–5   depends on the person specification. This example is for a personnel manager in a medium-sized voluntary organisation
    Page 6   standard except for details such as driving licence or languages and closing date

State that age criteria will not be taken into account in employment decisions.

Application for the post of:

PERSONNEL MANAGER

IMPORTANT:

The questions on this form have been designed to gain the information we need to assess your application against the person specification included in the package of materials sent out to you. Please do not include a general CV or other bulky background material.

Please try to fit all your answers on the form. We are keen that all applicants do themselves justice, so do use an extra sheet if you need more space for any answers. Please type or write clearly and, if possible, in black ink not in blue, which doesn't photocopy so well.

Application Number_____
[For organisation to complete]

NAME: *(allow 1 lines)*

ADDRESS: *(allow 5 lines)*

PHONE NUMBERS:
(day):   (evening):

EQUAL OPPORTUNITIES

Application Number_____

BRIEF HISTORY

Please list briefly the activities, training, paid or unpaid work and voluntary activities you have undertaken, starting with the most recent and working backwards. (Just summarise experience if it is not relevant to this post.)

Dates   Activity/Course/Job   Employer/Organisation/College

(allow 20 lines)

WORKING WITH PEOPLE

Please describe your previous experience of jobs or situations where you have had to motivate and support other people, and say what makes you think you are good at it.

(allow 10 lines)

What is your experience of teamwork?

(allow 10 lines)

PERSONNEL

Please give details of your experience of personnel work, including recruitment and selection tasks and staff supervision.

(allow 20 lines)

EQUAL OPPORTUNITIES

What experience have you had of implementing equal opportunities policies or dealing with oppression?

(allow 20 lines)

FACTS AND FIGURES

Please describe any experience you have had of book-keeping or of preparing budgets, financial reports or statistics or any qualification you have that might be relevant.

(allow 10 lines)

COMPUTER SKILLS

Please describe what wordprocessing skills you have. Include a rough estimate of words per minute and any packages you are familiar with.

(allow 10 lines)

PRACTICAL MATTERS

If you wish, please tell us about any aids or assistance that might help you to do the job. Information you provide will not jeopardise your application.

(allow 10 lines)

Please tell us any other information you think might be important or useful for us to know (e.g. if you need a work permit).

Do you have a full, valid UK driving licence?

[IF IT'S A JOB IN A RESTRICTED PROFESSION UNDER THE REHABILITATION OF OFFENDERS ACT, ask about previous convictions]

Please tell us about any specific assistance you might need for attending an interview on _____ _____ (We will in any case pay rail fares or car mileage equivalent and overnight accommodation up to £ . . . if necessary.)

REFEREES

Please give names and addresses (and daytime phone numbers if possible) of two referees, at least one of whom should be someone who can comment on your work, paid or unpaid. We will take up references only of the successful candidates, after the interview, and only with your permission.

1.   2.

DECLARATION

As far as I know, all the information I have given here is accurate.

Signed: Date:

*Please return this form to*_____*not later than*_____

2.3 ACTION SUMMARY

- collect relevant information for the job description
- decide on the best way to fill the job
- draw up a timetable for recruitment action
- consult on equality targets and action for recruitment
- draw up the job description, person specification, application form — consult as necessary

- decide on the recruitment methods to be used
- draw up the advert
- write the covering letter
- Brief the administration staff

THE APPLICATION FORM

Do

- include a section so that all candidates can include paid and unpaid experience (e.g. in the voluntary sector)

But remember, Don't

- include age-related criteria
- include questions about personal circumstances, for example relating to marital status or family responsibilities
- ask for hobbies or interests on the form

THE JOB DESCRIPTION

Do

- describe the requirements and duties of the job accurately
- describe those that are necessary and those that are done in conjunction with others if time permits

THE PERSON SPECIFICATION

Do

- produce a person specification of the essential and desirable skills, knowledge and abilities of the person required to carry out the job

But remember, Don't

- set standards higher than necessary
- set unnecessary education standards or specify British qualifications only
- include any personal circumstances in the person specification, such as age or marital status preferred

ADVERTISING

Do

- publicise vacancies wherever possible
- encourage applications from people of one sex or race where they have been underrepresented in the last 12 months
- place ads in places where a wide range of people will see them
- circulate vacancy lists to people with disabilities in your community through the local authority or other community networks
- encourage people with disabilities to apply where they are underrepresented in the workforce

But remember, Don't

- use wording or representations that could be taken to indicate a preference for one sex or the other or for one racial group
- recruit on the basis of word of mouth or friends or relatives of the current workforce

2.4 LEGAL SUMMARY

Race Relations Act 1976 (does not apply in Northern Ireland)
Sex Discrimination Act 1975 and Sex Discrimination (NI) Order 1976 and amendment Fair Employment (NI) Acts 1976 and 1989 and Fair Employment Monitoring Regulations (NI) 1989
These Acts define areas of discrimination and victimisation and set positive action measures for people of different ethnic and racial groups, women, married people, men and, in Northern Ireland, people of different religious or political persuasions.

Rehabilitation of Offenders Act 1974 and Exceptions Order 1975
Rehabilitation of Offenders (NI) Order 1978 and Exceptions Order 1979
These Acts allow offenders who have a 'spent' sentence not to declare it on an application form unless the application is for one of the exempt categories of jobs.

Trade Union and Labour Relations (Consolidation) Act 1992 makes it unlawful to discriminate against people who are or are not members of a trade union.

3 SELECTION

If you got your advertising and job package right, you will have several applicants to choose from. There is no "right" number. Some jobs attract only half a dozen people, others draw 50 or 60 and some get hundreds. However many you get, the principles in making your choice are the same.

There are many barriers to fair selection, but it is still possible to develop a system that works for equality. This chapter describes a set of systematic, formal procedures that are likely to result in best practice and be cost effective.

KEY CONCEPTS

- stereotyping
- prejudice
- unequal treatment
- suitability vs. acceptability
- assessment centres
- psychological tests

QUESTIONS ANSWERED

- what is prejudice and how can I avoid it?
- what if I get a gut reaction against the best person on paper?
- what is biodata? Is it a useful process of screening?
- how can I best shortlist from 100 candidates?
- are tests better than interviews?

CONTENTS

1: **Principles of equality selection**
   Prejudice
   Stereotyping
   Unequal treatment
   Gut reactions
   Action summary
2: **Screening and Shortlisting**
   Screening
   Biodata
   Why shortlist?
     Using positive action and affirmative action
     Ex-offenders
   Shortlisting
     Who should be on a panel?
   Procedures for shortlisting
     Preparation
     Meetings
     The shortlisting decision
     Documentation
     Informing candidates
     Informing those not shortlisted
     Information-giving session
   Action summary
3: **Assessment Methods**
   Selection methods
     Choosing
   Selection tests
     Are they valid?
     Potential discrimination
   Types of tests
     Performance simulation
     Psychological tests
     Group tests
     Assessment centres

Using selection tests
Interviews
Action summary
4: ***The interviewing procedure***
The aim
Interviews for people with disabilities
   Getting information from candidates
   Arrangements for the interview
   Briefing interviewers
Practicalities
   Timing
   Information
   Administration
   Venue preparation
Panel preparation
   Clear roles
   Questions
   Flexibility
   The structure of the interview
Asking the questions
   Examples of different types of questions
   Questions to avoid
   Listen and take notes
   Record the answers systematically
Action summary
5: ***Action summary***
6: ***Legal summary***

3.1 PRINCIPLES OF EQUALITY SELECTION

We make judgements about people all the time — people on the tube, people on the street, people we see in the pub or in our social life. This is natural and arises from an inbuilt and basic need to assess whether we are in a safe or dangerous situation.

Job selection should be consciously different. The main aim of selection is to use non-discriminatory assessment methods that will best predict which applicant will be the most successful if appointed.

The selection process provides many danger points where direct or indirect discrimination can be brought into play by the selector. Sometimes this may be deliberate; at other times it may be due to unconscious perceptions. Research from the EOC into fair selection carried out in 1988 documented many real instances of prejudices in selection and how even a panel of selectors can collude in discriminating against women and against other groups of people.

A report on *Racism and Recruitment* (Jenkins, 1986) made a distinction between employers' use of *suitability* and *acceptability* in selection criteria.

Selection criteria based on *suitability* (those we should be using) are:

- technically and functionally specific criteria of performance
- defined primarily by job requirements and measured by technical and educational qualifications

Selection criteria based on *acceptability* (on which too many people wrongly rely) are:

- not related to the job, e.g. manner and attitude, appearance, personality, maturity
- defined by looking for a person who will not cause management any problems and who will 'fit in'

The following example comes from the same research:

> *Domestic responsibilities* for men are viewed as positive because they are believed to indicate stability and motivation, but negatively for women because they are believed to indicate divided loyalties between home and work.

These guidelines are designed to help you to avoid bias in selection arising from **prejudice, stereotyping, unequal treatment,** and **gut reactions.**

PREJUDICE

> *Preferences, attitudes, judgements and opinions formed without adequate knowledge or reason.*

If you make your decision on the basis of personal preference or opinion, you may well exclude someone from a job they would be perfectly good at. You should try not to have a fixed idea about how a job should be done or who would be suitable for it. You should base your decision *only* on whether the person has the right capability.

STEREOTYPING

> *A generalisation — often derogatory and based on prejudice — about any group. It can be used to prejudge a whole group on the basis of one individual and it can transfer one person's preconceived views of a group onto individual members of that group.*

Stereotyping means that you *assume* things about people because they belong to a particular group. For example, some people still believe that women with children are 'unreliable', and they are less likely to employ them for that reason. But are women with children less reliable?

For example:
One woman manager in the information technology business, a single parent, says 'We all leave at the same time, 7pm, only they go to the pub and I go home to put my child to bed. Which of us is more productive the next day, I wonder?'

Remember that you are trying to give people equal opportunity, so you should treat each person as an individual.

UNEQUAL TREATMENT

> *Unfair or unequal treatment of individuals because of their identity, e.g. gender, race, ethnic group, age*

Do not ask questions about people's ethnic origin or that of their family, or how they would react to a supervisor of a different race or sex, or whether they would be able to work with lesbians or gay men, or other similar questions.

For example:
In the information technology industry, recently one woman was puzzled by the long wait between applying for a job as a security manager with a computer firm and being appointed. After joining the company she discovered that, although the directors had thought her application the best out of the first batch from the agency, they'd been so reluctant to appoint a woman that they'd not only interviewed all the male agency candidates but advertised the post before being convinced.

GUT REACTIONS

Our perceptions of new people are conditioned by our history, upbringing, sex, race, class and culture and are highly subjective. Once we have recognised the operation of these deeply embedded psychological processes, we can learn to overcome them.

Distortions of perception are particularly likely when we meet people of a different social background, culture or gender from our own. In selection, gut reaction is not evidence on which to base long-term employment decisions.

The perception effects listed below, observed under test conditions, have been shown to affect the performance of selectors.

ASSUMED SIMILARITY EFFECT

When an interviewer establishes common ground with the candidate in certain ways that may be irrelevant to the job and generalises this to other areas, which may be selection criteria, this reinforces a tendency to recruit in one's own image.

For example:
Because you play rugby, you may show a preference for a candidate who has put on their CV that they play rugby.

Black candidates and women are not going to benefit from the 'Assumed Similarity Effect' where the selector is male and white.

PRIMACY EFFECT

The 'Primacy Effect' allows the first impression to influence the overall judgement of the candidate. For example, if the candidate gives a poor answer to a question on the first topic area, or has a real weakness in one area, it does not mean that they do not have good experience in other areas.

HALO EFFECT

The 'Halo Effect' allows a favourable impression of one trait to influence the judgement of other traits.

ACTION SUMMARY

- review the importance of getting the best person for the job (see the Introduction to the book and the introductions to Chapters 1 and 2)
- get training that confronts your own prejudices and potentially discriminatory practices. See the Address section in Chapter 8 for addresses of organisations that may be able to advise you on this.

Do

- ask all candidates the same questions — do not ask discriminatory questions
- decide on the basis of information given and the ability to do the job

But remember, Don't

- make assumptions
- ask discriminatory questions

3.2 SCREENING AND SHORTLISTING

Once you have a pile of application forms on your desk in response to the advert, how do you go about deciding which people will be on the shortlist?

SCREENING

Some employers receive so many applications that they feel unable to shortlist in the normal sense. They apply an initial screening process to weed out those not suitable for further assessment. This can be as arbitrary and ad hoc as taking every tenth form, or throwing them up in the air and seeing which ones land on the desk! One method of screening that claims to be more scientific is Biodata.

BIODATA

This method is where a set of personal data is screened so that those candidates that best match the ideal in terms of personal factors such as age, sex, area lived in, hobbies and mortgage are selected to go on to the next stage. This method is particularly questionable in equal opportunities practice.

Some firms use the profile of the existing workforce as the standard for a successful match. This seems a highly dubious method of selection as it tends to replicate the existing workforce profile and hence indirectly discriminates against those not already or poorly represented. This could be particularly discriminatory if applied in Northern Ireland, where areas tend to be highly segregated along religious belief lines.

The best method, however tedious, is always to shortlist on the basis of detailed skill-based

person specifications not personality-based criteria.

WHY SHORTLIST?

The purpose of shortlisting is to decide who you want to interview or assess by some other means. Shortlisting should be carried out on the basis of the information supplied on application forms and possibly other documentation that you have asked for, such as examples of design materials.

Application forms are to be preferred to CVs because then the same information is available on all candidates, not just what they have chosen to put on their CVs. They also avoid judgements about the presentation of a CV, which may not be a very efficient predictor of success in any particular post.

Even if you have only a few applicants, it is still worth making a shortlist to avoid interviewing people who have no chance of getting the job.

USING POSITIVE ACTION AND AFFIRMATIVE ACTION

If you have taken positive or affirmative action measures under the Race Relations Act, Sex Discrimination Act or Fair Employment Act (in Northern Ireland), then you are still not allowed to discriminate at the point of selection. Once the applications arrive on your desk you must treat them all in the same way.

Only when you have used a Genuine Occupational Qualification (see Chapter 1) for a male or female or a member of a particular ethnic group can you stick to shortlisting people of that race or sex only.

EX-OFFENDERS

If you have asked for information about ex-offenders on the application form, do not de-select anyone who has a conviction that is not relevant to the post, providing that the post is not one of those exempt under the Rehabilitation of Offenders Act (see Chapter 7).

SHORTLISTING PANELS

As a line manager, you may be the only person responsible for carrying out shortlisting of applicants. However, it generally makes good sense to involve more than one person in the process because:

- decisions are more likely to be objective if made by more than one person
- it is in accordance with guidance by CRE, FEC, EOC and IPM. (On the advantages and disadvantages of selection panels versus individual interviews, see the section on assessment methods below.)

WHO SHOULD BE ON A PANEL?

The panel should be drawn mainly from appropriate senior staff relevant to the level of post to be filled or board members. An outside specialist should be included only if the relevant expertise is not otherwise available. A major priority should be for people with the relevant knowledge and expertise to be present on the panel, regardless of other considerations.

It is very easy to introduce discrimination at this stage, even without meaning to, so, ideally, all members of a selection panel should have been trained in equal opportunities selection and in interviewing principles and techniques. If this is not possible, then at least one person should be trained. Good quality equal opportunities training should focus on the effects that generalised assumptions and prejudices can have on selection decisions.

All members of the panel should participate in preparing for the selection interview, including the shortlisting of candidates and the preparation of questions for interview.

PROCEDURES FOR SHORTLISTING

PREPARATION

If the panel has been formed early enough, it will have played a part in drawing up the person specification and application form. If not, at least make sure that everyone on the panel has a copy of the job package so that they can familiarise themselves with it beforehand.

If there are people on the panel without training, make sure that they know what is expected of them and have read through the sections in this handbook on selection and interviewing.

MEETINGS

Shortlisting should ideally be done in a meeting, so that people can discuss any disagreements about particular candidates. However, if it is difficult for everyone to meet it is sometimes possible for people to draw up their shortlists individually and then discuss disagreements over the phone.

THE SHORTLISTING DECISION

The **essential criteria** from the person specification form the basis of shortlisting. New criteria or changes to criteria should not be made at the shortlisting stage.

Give each panel member a checklist with the names or numbers of the applicants and the list of criteria you are looking for. They each go through the application forms and fill in their assessments on the checklist. They can then compare notes and discuss any disagreements.

No applicant should be rejected on the basis of assumptions about the relative abilities of men and women, or ability related to race or age, or any criterion that does not appear on the person specification. This is where anonymous application forms are particularly useful, as they remove any temptation to make judgements on the basis of names.

> **Case law**
> Webster v. Kirklees Metropolitan Council. A white man who was not shortlisted for a council racial equal opportunities post was discriminated against on racial grounds. The tribunal found that some of the white male applicants (none of whom were shortlisted) were just as well qualified as those who were shortlisted.
>
> The tribunal also found that the selection procedure had been open to abuse as one of the panel members had failed to 'declare an interest' and had shortlisted people known to them.

Declare an interest

Always ask panel members if they know any of the applicants personally or by reputation. In this case they should 'declare an interest' and ideally not be involved in the decision to interview or appoint. If this is not possible, say because of the nature of the field of expertise, then very clear rules of conduct must be adhered to in the decision-making process. For example, try to bring in an outsider who definitely doesn't know anyone, or have any 'axe to grind', to balance the panel and ensure favouritism does not result. There should be absolutely no discussion of any person's reputed qualities or anecdotal evidence of performance in previous posts, unless there is a real basis for accepting these as fact. Even then, such information must be treated with circumspection.

If lots of applicants fully meet all the essential criteria in the person specification, then use the **desirable criteria** to shorten the list.

If this still results in more than eight applicants being shortlisted, then your person specification criteria are set too low and need revising for the next recruitment. Meanwhile, you could try to see all the shortlisted applicants for a short preliminary interview to attempt to cut down the applicants for a second in-depth interview. If this is still an impossibly large number, then the fairest course of action is to readvertise using new person specification criteria and to explain to current applicants that they can choose to re-submit their applications, bearing in mind the new criteria.

If you have the opposite problem of no one meeting all the essential criteria, then you can choose either to readvertise using lower criteria or to interview all those who meet most of the criteria and offer training to bring them up to the standard of the person specification once in post. You then have to be careful not to de-select the applicants at the decision-making stage just because they didn't meet a particular criterion.

Any applicant with a disability who meets all the essential criteria in the person specification should be interviewed regardless of any requirement to adapt buildings or facilities if they are successful. Grants may be available from the government for this purpose. Check with the Training Commission and Disablement Advisory Service for further details.

> **Case law**
> A Roman Catholic nurse accepted record damages of £30,000 in a religious discrimination case against a Northern Ireland Health Authority.
> The Health Board applied different shortlisting criteria to her application than to those of Protestant applicants. All three available posts were filled by Protestants, two of whom would not have met the shortlisting criteria that had been applied to the Roman Catholic Nurse's application.
> (Fair Employment (Northern Ireland) Act 1989)

DOCUMENTATION

The reasons for rejection and success should be documented on special recruitment monitoring forms designed for the purpose. Record the assessments and decisions of shortlisting panels in relation to the relevant factors and their importance.

The Fair Employment (Northern Ireland) Act requires that all application forms and related materials are retained for 12 months after the interview date in order for any subsequent complaints about the implementation of selection decisions to be dealt with. There is also an obligation to retain certain specific information about applicants for monitoring purposes for three years.

In England and Wales, all relevant forms should be kept for 12 months in case they are needed as evidence at a tribunal.

If the recruitment has worked so far according to equal opportunities, the shortlist should produce a range of people who have had an equal chance of inclusion. If most of the applicants were women, but most of the shortlist are men, for example, then you might suspect that something is wrong with your process, and take action to investigate further.

INFORMING CANDIDATES

Inform all shortlisted candidates of the decision as soon as possible after shortlisting. Tell them:

- the format of the selection process, including interview, assessment centre or tests
- the interview dates and time of the interview
- the number of interviewers and who they are, their jobs or roles
- what they need to bring, if anything
- an idea of the range of question areas
- how long the interview will last
- information about travel expenses (IPM recommends paying reasonable and significant expenses incurred by applicants attending interviews)
- access details for people with disabilities

(See the sample letter on p. 91.)

INFORMING THOSE NOT SHORTLISTED

It is good practice to inform people that they have not been shortlisted rather than to leave them hanging on, not knowing. It may not always be practicable to do so, but every effort should be made.

The letter should also give applicants the name and phone number of a person to contact if further information is required. (See the sample letter on p. 90.)

> *You are not obliged to give information about why people are not shortlisted. However, if someone with qualifications better than those of other people who were put on the shortlist takes you to a tribunal and complains of discrimination, then they will stand a good chance of winning, unless you can demonstrate that you took other legitimate factors into account. Even if they had been shortlisted and had still not got the job because there was an undeniably better-qualified candidate, you have still deprived them of the opportunity of going for the job and so have committed unlawful discrimination.*

The legality of whether or not you have to tell people why they were not shortlisted is a difficult one. If you are applying fair selection procedures then there should be no problem. However, discrimination does sometimes creep in at the shortlisting stage and candidates are right to be aware of that. If you are not applying fair selection procedures, then you are open to being taken to an industrial tribunal on the basis of direct or indirect discrimination.

Sample letter to those not shortlisted

Date

Dear [NAME]

JOB TITLE

The selection panel have carefully considered your application for the post of [job title], and have unfortunately decided not to shortlist you for interview.

Should you require further details of the decision please contact [name] on [phone], who will be happy to talk to you about the reasons for the panel's decision. Or they will send you a note of the decision in writing, should you wish it.

I wish you success in any future applications you may be making.

Yours sincerely,

Chair of the selection panel

Sample letter to those shortlisted

Date

Dear [NAME]

JOB TITLE

The selection panel have carefully considered your application for the post of [job title], and would like to invite you for interview.

The interview will take place in our offices at . . . am on . . . .

Please let me know as soon as possible if this time is convenient for you. It may be possible to swap times for a later/earlier interview with another candidate.

The interview will last for approximately 1 hour; there will be three interviewers taken from members of staff and . . . .

The question areas will cover in more detail how you meet the criteria on the person specification.

[*Optional, where appropriate*

There will also be a short test in the form of . . . .

We would like you to bring any copies of magazines you have designed
[Or some other relevant request for materials]

We would like you to attend a one-day Assessment Centre at . . . .]

The offices are fully accessible, car parking is/is not available 50m from the front entrance, space for

> setting down is available outside our front entrance, the nearest tube is . . . .
>
> 2nd class railfare costs will be reimbursed and the organisation will contribute to overnight accommodation costs incurred and additional caring costs incurred if necessary to the amount of £ . . . .
>
> Please confirm to [name] at [office] that you can attend at the time specified above.
>
> I look forward to meeting you.
>
> Yours sincerely,
>
> Manager

INFORMATION-GIVING SESSION

Any information-giving sessions or services provided for the benefit of shortlisted candidates must be fair to all. It should be made clear that information-giving is separate from the selection process.

There is a significant problem with using informal procedures in a process that is supposed to be formalised. However careful you are, impressions are bound to be given, and there may be a comeback on those making selection decisions.

ACTION SUMMARY

- always try to shortlist and not screen candidates
- draw up shortlisting criteria based on person specification
- draw up a shortlisting checklist form
- select a representative, and preferably trained, panel
- shortlist on the basis of criteria, not assumptions
- make sure all applicants get equal treatment
- be clear about why candidates are not selected
- keep forms and records of decisions for 12 months in case of tribunal, and for three years for FEC monitoring purposes
- organise acceptance and rejection letters quickly

Do

- stick to the agreed person specification criteria (skill based)
- ignore all material you haven't asked for in applications
- ignore all photographs sent
- declare if you have a personal interest in a candidate
- shortlist systematically
- keep a record of your decisions and the reasons for them

But remember, Don't

- use biodata to screen applicants
- select the best laid out CV or the neatest handwriting
- take irrelevant personal details into account, such as colour of tie, length of hair, nature of make-up, number of dependants
- create an image of the 'ideal' person for the job in terms of age, sex, ethnic group, physical ability, etc.

3.3 METHODS OF ASSESSMENT

You need to be clear about the best methods to assess your selection criteria at the recruitment stage.

Focus primarily on job-related criteria that can be objectively assessed, and you will be heading for the best possible outcome.

Even if there are 'personality traits' that you think are necessary for effective performance, such as flexibility or innovation, make sure that a test is used that may in some way be more objective than your own gut feelings about whether someone will fit in. (Review the section on the principles of equality selection above.)

Make sure that your methods do not directly discourage or discriminate against people with disabilities. The way some tests are carried out may disadvantage some people because of factors that have nothing to do with whether they can do the job.

For example:

- *make sure there is enough light in the interview or test for partially sighted people to be able to see as clearly as they can.*

- *remove any unnecessary time constraints on completion of tests.*

SELECTION METHODS

There is a variety of methods of assessing candidates for suitability against person specification criteria:

- application form
- tests — job related
    psychological
    group
    assessment centres
- interview

The application form and interview concentrate on what a candidate has done in the past and attempt to extrapolate from this evidence the degree to which they will be successful in the future.

Selection devices like job-related tests, where relevant, may be a better predictor because they sample present behaviour or skills in order to predict future behaviour.

CHOOSING

The choice of selection methods is likely to depend on a number of factors:

- **Time** The post may have to be filled quickly (however, it is costly to make long-term decisions for short-term reasons).

- **Cost** Tests and assessment centres may be more reliable but validation before initial use involves a lot of time and energy. They are only for the medium to large employer.

- **Ease** Interviews and job-related performance tests are easier to devise and set up, although training needs to be carried out first.

- **Staff involved in selection** Do they have the training and ability to carry out the interview or assessment centre?

- **Appropriateness** Beware of putting good people off. Senior staff may resent doing an intelligence test.

- **Validity** The British Psychological Society quotes predictive validity coefficients of 0.25 for structured interviews and 0 for unplanned interviews. These figures mean that interviews are only 25% more accurate than picking names out of a hat.

   Job simulation exercises (see below) achieve the best validity rating among selection techniques and a combination of different techniques achieves the highest rating of all.

Using a variety of methods gives the best result as it allows individuals to shine in different areas.

SELECTION TESTS

ARE THEY VALID?

All tests must be a valid predictor of the ability to do the job. Hence all tests must be 'normed' by reference to success in the job for which applicants' suitability is to be checked. This requires a relevant trial group of several hundred. Unless a statistically significant relationship can be demonstrated between test scores and job performance, the test should not be used as a basis for selection decisions.

Some tests may therefore not be suitable for use in small organisations where there are small numbers of people performing different tasks.

POTENTIAL DISCRIMINATION

There has been much debate about the degree to which tests are proof from accusations of unfair discrimination against minority groups and women. It would thus be best to take specialist advice from the personnel department or a reputable consultancy group before considering using tests.

Do selection tests contain unjustifiable cultural bias? In some cases they may do where a job applicants' first language is not English or where they were educated outside the country.

The CRE Code of Practice on Racial Discrimination says:

Selection tests which contain irrelevant questions or exercises on matters which may be unfamiliar to racial minority applicants should not be used (for example general knowledge questions on matters more likely to be familiar to the indigenous population).

Using a test developed by a professional industrial psychologist trained in psychometrics and carried out with the correct administration is not sufficient to prove that no unfair discrimination has taken place. In addition to the validation process, you need to norm the test on ethnic minority workers. This will be difficult when the ethnic minority population is small in the workforce.

A 1990 CRE report into London Underground's use of selection tests (*Lines of Progress*) concludes:

Our report draws attention to the use of psychological tests for job selection in a multi-racial labour market, and demonstrates that employers cannot assume that a generally reliable test will be equally reliable for a particular population or for a particular job. They must first check if the tests were designed for and tried out on a similarly diverse population and if the results had a racially discriminatory pattern. Second, employers must make sure that the tests measure precisely the skills and abilities needed for the job. Any mismatch here will mean inefficient and possibly discriminatory selection.

TYPES OF TESTS

Tests can be divided broadly into four main types:

- psychological tests
- group tests
- tests that simulate the performance of real job tasks
- assessment centres

PSYCHOLOGICAL TESTS

Aptitude tests Tests of aptitude are supposed to measure the individual's ability to develop in either specific or general terms. However it is important to remember that there is not necessarily a high correlation between a high aptitude test score and a high degree of job performance because motivation and other factors play a part in real job situations.

Aptitude tests are usually grouped into two categories — those measuring general mental ability or intelligence and those measuring specific abilities or aptitudes.

- *Intelligence tests* are designed to give a measure of overall mental ability. A variety of questions are usually included such as verbal ability, mental reasoning, similarities, opposites, vocabulary, number work and general knowledge and spatial ability. Evidence seems to suggest that women on average score less well than men on the spatial ability component of the tests. For this reason employers using such tests would have to show that spatial ability was a key skill in job performance.

    General knowledge can be highly culture specific as well, so care needs to be taken about the validation for a diverse workforce.

- *Special aptitude tests* cover a range of tests in specific areas, such as verbal ability, spatial ability, manual dexterity and so on. Some tests concentrate on mechanical ability acquired from work experience. This may discriminate against women as they generally have less mechanical input in education and upbringing. Aptitude tests are available that focus on the level of inherent skill rather than on acquired skill.

- *Trainability tests* are used to measure potential ability to be trained, usually for mechanical or craft work. The test involves people doing a practical task that they have not done before, after being 'trained' how to do it. The test measures how well they responded to the training, but this depends a bit on how well the 'training' is carried out.

Personality tests Personality tests are generally not recommended in selection as they are not dependent on suitability criteria related to the job performance. It is easy to use these tests to justify recruiting people with certain personality traits that meet selectors' preconceptions of the 'ideal' candidate, who is not necessarily the best person for the job.

GROUP SELECTION TESTS

The group is either set a task or given a topic to discuss or negotiate and then observed by the selectors. It is imperative that you train the observers.

PERFORMANCE SIMULATION

To avoid the criticism and potential liability of psychological, aptitude and other written tests, there is increasing interest in the development of tests that simulate performance. These require the applicant to carry out specific tasks that have been shown or are believed to be key for doing the job successfully.

Simulation tests You may create a simulated problem or situation in which the candidate's competence in dealing with a specific part of the job is evaluated. For example, you could ask prospective clerical assistants to do a filing exercise, or require prospective managers to prioritise the items in a typical morning's In Tray and say what they would do with each item.

Attainment tests These test the attainment of standards in practical or knowledge skills necessary for the job. For example:

- typing tests
- questionnaires on specific bodies of knowledge required at fingertips
- trade skills
- machine or computer operating skills

Presentations You may ask candidates to give a short presentation to the panel based on information you have previously supplied. This is particularly useful in evaluating a candidate's ability to group complex information and draw out the crucial points, their ability to communicate and their ability to argue a case.

Such a presentation should be used only in selecting for posts that require formal or informal presentations to be made on a regular basis.

ASSESSMENT CENTRES

An assessment centre is a set of performance simulation tests (some group, some individual) specifically designed to evaluate a candidate's skills and competencies, their suitability for particular jobs and their potential for development. Applicants are appraised by trained personnel workers, occupational psychologists or line managers.

As the exercises are generally designed to simulate the work that managers actually do, they tend to be more accurate predictors of later job performance. This explains the huge increase in the use of assessment centres in the last few years.

However, they are expensive and, like all assessment methods, they carry the inbuilt human factors of error. They may also be counterproductive if the wrong competencies are assessed or if there are flaws in the assessment process.

Validation Very thorough analysis should be carried out, of both the process itself and its outcomes, before a commitment is made to an ongoing programme of centres. The factors to consider in validating a centre include:

- the assessor's and participant's immediate views
- whether the assessments make sense to the participants' line managers and are confirmed by other evidence
- in the longer term, whether the assessment predictions come true
- whether any test or exercise was hard to rate or administer or failed to differentiate between participants.

USING SELECTION TESTS

You must ask some very searching questions before you use any selection test, either one you have devised yourself or one bought in from a company.

- will it provide any extra useful information on the criteria on the person specification?
- is it appropriate to use a test at all?

If you do decide to use a test:

- use professionally designed tests
- check the suitability of the test for the job under consideration, using a thorough job description as the basis
- consider how the test will be administered, especially how it will be scored and interpreted
- train staff in the administration of tests, but be aware that most psychometric tests should be scored and validated only by fully trained people, usually a psychologist
- follow the administration instructions to the letter
- make sure the environment where the tests are to be taken is suitable, especially for people with disabilities
- try and establish a relaxed atmosphere beforehand
- check that candidates understand the instructions
- provide examples for them to see beforehand
- note whether or not the timing of the test is significant and inform candidates
- if a test requires a particular strategy to score well, advise participants of this — e.g. advise them to leave questions that cannot be answered quickly and come back to them
- validate tests separately for men and women and different ethnic minorities — this should be done by a qualified individual
- if professional validation is not possible: Compare the average test scores for men with the

average test scores for women on the same tests. Compare the rejection rates for men and women and different minority groups. Investigate any marked differences

- check whether a higher percentage of one sex or racial group fails to be shortlisted or appointed despite high test scores.
- limit the confidentiality of results
- feed back results to candidates

Remember:

- use only tests that actually measure attributes defined as selection criteria.
- tests designed by professionals MUST have been developed and validated so that they don't discriminate against women, people from different ethnic groups and people with disabilities.
- a single test is of only limited value in assessing the ability of a person to do a job.
- avoid timed tests if untimed ones are available.

For assessment centres

- train assessors in the avoidance of bias or make sure that the outside company's assessors are trained.
- use rating scales on specific items or aspects of the candidates' work in the marking of paper exercises rather than a general mark for the work as a whole.

- refer to the candidates by number where possible so that assessors are unaware of the race and sex profile of candidates when marking a paper.

INTERVIEWS

Surveys on the use of interviews have concluded that the reliability and validity of interviews are generally low. A review of the research shows the following disadvantages:

- prior knowledge about the applicant will bias an interviewer's evaluation
- an interviewer has a stereotype of what constitutes a 'good' applicant
- an interviewer tends to favour applicants who share their own attitudes
- the order in which applicants are interviewed will influence evaluations
- the order in which information is elicited will influence evaluations
- negative information is given unduly high weight
- an interviewer comes to a decision very early on in the interview
- an interviewer forgets much of the content of the interview minutes after it's finished

However, despite their drawbacks, interviews are still widely used and it is important to maximise their benefit to the organisation. They are therefore dealt with in some detail in the next section.

ACTION SUMMARY

- record the various factors considered relevant to a particular job in the person specification before the shortlisting, interviewing and selection of candidates

- decide on the relative importance to be given to each factor at all stages of selection — shortlisting, assessment and decision

- satisfy yourself that these factors and their relative importance are justifiable, appropriate to the job and clearly objective

- record the assessments and decisions of the shortlisting, interviewing and selection panels in relation to the relevant factors and their importance (a simple marking chart can be helpful)

- retain all records for monitoring, in case of any subsequent complaint and legal obligation

Do

- choose methods to match the selection criteria you have identified

- remember that job-related simulations are the best predictor

- ensure that those making the selection are clearly informed of the criteria

- give training on sound selection procedures

3.4 THE INTERVIEWING PROCEDURE

THE AIM

The aim of the interview is to:

- extract the relevant information in enough detail to be able to make a decision, i.e.
  - fill in the gaps on the application form
  - explore the candidate's motivation and attitudes
  - give the candidate sufficient information about the job and the organisation so that they can make a decision
  - give the candidate a fair hearing

- develop rapport — but not be blinded by it
  Giving a good reception and non-verbal encouragement when appropriate will help build the relationship and also make the candidate less nervous and more willing to talk about their strengths and weaknesses.

The main way to achieve these goals is to develop a questioning technique that elicits the relevant information to make a non-discriminatory decision.

INTERVIEWS FOR PEOPLE WITH DISABILITIES

There are three main areas to be aware of:

- getting information from the candidates
- the arrangements for the interview
- briefing the interviewers

GETTING INFORMATION FROM CANDIDATES

Ask on the application form (see the example in Chapter 2), if candidates have any special needs at interview. However, many people with disabilities may not disclose information at this stage for fear of being rejected out of hand.

If they get an interview, anyone who needs special facilities will probably ask then, but you could ask again in the covering letter that you send out inviting them to interview.

Inform all applicants about physical access to the building, parking facilities and how close they are, communication assistance such as signing or interpreting.

ARRANGEMENTS FOR THE INTERVIEW

Briefing the candidates in the normal way should be enough, but pay special attention to letting the reception staff know if anyone is coming with an interpreter or needs special assistance in finding the venue for the interview.

The room will need to be:

- big enough to allow people in wheelchairs or on crutches to manoeuvre
- light enough to facilitate lip reading (interviewers should face the light)

BRIEFING INTERVIEWERS

Inform interviewers if there are any blind or deaf people coming so that they can sit facing the light, make sure that they speak clearly and communicate even more clearly than usual.

Be very aware of any interviewer making assumptions about a person's ability to do any aspect of the job. Ask the candidate in detail if you need to know.

Check with candidates themselves if they would need special equipment or adaptations. They know their own boundaries to action far better than any interviewer at first meeting.

PANEL VERSUS INDIVIDUAL INTERVIEWS

Panel interviews are recommended. The arguments for and against are as follows:

INDIVIDUAL INTERVIEWS

Advantages	*Disadvantages*
Easier to establish rapport	Important points can be missed
Less intimidating (esp. for school leavers)	May be subjective
More flexible	Not recommended by equality bodies
Can set own pace and direction	Only one opinion available
Relatively cheap	Sole rep for organisation
Easy to organise	

PANEL INTERVIEWS

Advantages	*Disadvantages*
Help ensure equal opportunities policy is followed	Less control over time
	More organisation needed
Other panel members can pick up points missed by one interviewer	More preparation time needed
	May be intimidating for the candidate

Panel can share opinions on assessment (beware collusion)	Potential for conflict between panel members
Questions and decisions more objective	Problems of panel boredom for those not actually interviewing
Can bring in a technical expert	
May give a better feel to the organisation	

PRACTICALITIES

Good panel interviewing requires a systematic, well-organised approach. The practicalities of organising good interviews are complex but procedural. Once a code of practice and a method have been worked out, then they simply need sticking to.

TIMING

Plan the length and timings of the interview. Allow plenty of time in between for run on, for the interviewers to fill in their assessment sheets, and for coffee breaks.

INFORMATION

Inform the shortlisted candidates of the time and place of the interview, the panel size, if they need to bring anything, the expected length of the interview, expenses.

Contact people with special needs before the interview and make arrangements for them.

Send prior information to the panel in good time. Interviewers will need:

- the application forms
- the job description

- an interview checklist/person specification
- prepared questions
  - job centred
  - person centred
- details regarding terms and conditions

ADMINISTRATION

Decide who will take care of answering the door, welcoming candidates, talking to them, seeing round the premises, dealing with expenses, and showing them out.

Make sure there is someone on reception to take messages, and decide if the interviews can be interrupted under any circumstances or not.

VENUE PREPARATION

Coming to your offices or the venue you have chosen for the interview may be the first physical contact an applicant has had with the organisation. It is important to give a good impression and to convey the idea that you have thought about their comfort and sorted out practical details to ensure that the interview goes as smoothly as possible. Here are some pointers:

- minimise the formality of the interview room
- make sure someone is there to let people in, get them a cup of coffee and deal with expenses and travel arrangements
- have a separate waiting area, with papers or leaflets about the organisation
- put up warning notices to other staff that the interview room is in use

- ensure the interviews are not interrupted by phone calls, etc.

PANEL PREPARATION

The selection panel should meet in advance of the interview to decide:

- the roles of each member
- a clear plan of the shape of the interview
- question areas
- specific sample questions
- who should ask which ones
- the beginning and ending

CLEAR ROLES

The panel should allocate roles among the interviewers. The most important role is that of chairperson. Other roles might be timekeeping and seeing out.

Role of the chair

- makes the introductions
- explains the process of interview
- tells the candidate if they can ask questions on the way through or at the end
- moves the questioning on
- keeps the flow going
- keeps the interview to time

- deals with problems or irrelevances
- chairs the responses to the applicants' questions
- closes the interview and tells the candidate what will happen next
- chairs the decision-making discussion after the interview

QUESTIONS

The interview panel should draw up a framework of questions that applies to all candidates. These might cover:

- their current job or activity
- what particularly interests them about the job they are applying for
- skills and experience: expanding from the application form
- how the candidate might apply them in the job
- asking how particular situations might be tackled or how they tackled a particular event

The question areas should be divided up according to expertise among the panel members and certain common questions agreed beforehand. Each candidate will have different skills and experience and therefore will need probing on different areas. These should be decided before each candidate is interviewed.

Candidates should be questioned in a similar way under each area. However, the panel should agree a procedure for other interviewers wishing to follow on from the main questioner on a particular topic. Prepare a standard sheet for the interview with standard questions and a space for individual points for discussion. Each panel member should have a copy of the sheet in order to make notes while the interviews are taking place.

All questions must be clearly related to job requirements (as described in the person specification). The substance of questions must not vary according to the perceived ethnic or national origins, disability, marital status, sexuality, age or any other characteristics attributed to the candidate. Candidates should not be asked questions about their personal circumstances or family commitments.

Where a job involves unsocial or irregular hours or travel, the full facts must be presented in the job information to all applicants before the interview. The selection panel must establish by a simple question whether or not each candidate has understood the requirements of the job. Questions about domestic obligations should not be asked as they could be construed as showing bias against women.

FLEXIBILITY

It is more important to gain the relevant information than to ask only set questions. Some candidates may need supplementary or probing questions, and their answers might lead along different paths in each case.

THE STRUCTURE OF THE INTERVIEW

Each interview should begin by introducing the candidate to the panel and end by inviting the candidate to ask questions or clarify any issues that arose during the interview. The procedure and timescale for informing candidates of the decision should then be explained.

ASKING THE QUESTIONS

An interview is a nerve-racking situation for any candidate and for interviewers. Care therefore needs to be taken to put the candidate at their ease and to ask an easy introductory question to get things going. An open and frank attitude should be taken towards any people with disabilities.

- take care to speak clearly and directly and to explain any questions that are not understood

- make sure that candidates have an opportunity to ask their own questions

- before the interview ends, all selection panel members must be sure that they have sufficient information for the assessment of all criteria

- ask as many open but specific questions as possible

EXAMPLES OF DIFFERENT TYPES OF QUESTIONS

Rapport-building questions These will allow the candidate to talk on areas that they feel confident about.

'Tell us the aspect you enjoyed most of your last job.'
'What are the main responsibilities of your current job?'

Open questions These encourage the candidate to talk.

'Describe a situation in which . . .'
'Why did you leave college?'

Probing questions When you want to probe a certain skill area it is better not to ask a hypothetical question but to ask about how they have actually handled the particular experience themselves. Don't let a vague or general uninformative answer pass without a probing question to make the candidate give more detailed evidence.

'When you produced final accounts, what form did they take?'

'Exactly what percentage of your time is spent in training?'

Closed questions These tend to produce Yes or No answers and have limited use on very specific criteria.

'Do you have a driving licence?'
'When did you join the pension fund?'

Linking questions These improve the flow of the interview and show listening skills.

'Earlier you described a difficult person you had to deal with, could you now tell me which areas of supervision you find most challenging?'

Summaries These give a sense of purpose and pace in the interview and are helpful in long interviews and at the end of an interview.

'So, over the past three years you have operated two different types of word processor and trained four other members of staff to use them. How do you think you could use this skill in this job?'

QUESTIONS TO AVOID

- **Avoid stereotypes and generalisations about a person's perceived culture**

    'Our supporters are mainly white and middle class; do you think being black will affect your ability to work with them?'

    'You worked in an all-women team in your last job; will you be able to work with men?'

- **Avoid questions about domestic intentions and arrangements**

    Where it is necessary to assess how personal circumstances will affect performance of the job, discuss this objectively without making assumptions about marital status, children and domestic obligations.

> **Case law**
> Woodhead case. The real issue in deciding whether questions are discriminatory or not must be based on what the employer needs to know. The issue is that the candidate is aware of the constraints of the job and can make effective plans to work within them. Employers do not need to know what those plans are nor should they make assumptions about the viability of those plans.

Ask:

> 'You will sometimes have to work until 7pm at short notice. Will you be able to do that?'

rather than

> 'What arrangements will you be able to make to look after your children if you have to work late?'

- **Avoid questions about trade union activities**

    The interviewer may respond to questions from the interviewee regarding trade unions. The interviewer should state categorically that membership or non-membership of a trade union is nothing to do with the selection process.

- **Avoid multiple questions**

    'How many years have you worked at organisation and what were the main responsibilities of your job there and what did you enjoy most about it?'

- **Avoid too many hypothetical questions**

    This type of question needs to be asked with care. It is unfair to expect a candidate to give a detailed answer on an area where they do not have the technical knowledge. But some questions of this nature can be illuminating:

    'What would you do if a person made a sexist comment in a group you were leading?'

- **Avoid leading questions**

    Such questions appear to be looking for a particular answer and are pointless.

    'You gained most of your equal opportunities experience in your last job did you?'

- **Avoid dwelling on a candidate's weaknesses**

    'It's a shame you don't have any relevant selling experience.'

- **Avoid answering your own questions**

    'How long did you work in your last job — three years was it?'

LISTEN AND TAKE NOTES

All members of the panel should listen carefully to the candidate's answers. Each interviewer should make brief notes of the candidate's rating on each point during the interview in the form of: Not met, Partly met, Fully met.

RECORD THE ANSWERS SYSTEMATICALLY

Interviewers must keep notes in order to make fair comparisons between candidates when deciding. They must fully record their rating of the candidate on the prepared form after each interview.

ACTION SUMMARY

- make suitable arrangements for any candidates with disabilities prior to the interview
- arrange for candidates to be assessed by a panel rather than by one person alone
- avoid very short interviews: extending them from 15 to 30 minutes avoids interviewers coming to a premature decision
- avoid spending too long on the earlier part of the interview and then run out of time to probe as thoroughly as is needed on the key issues of how well the candidate will perform the tasks
- base assessments upon factual evidence of past performance, behaviour and achievements
- make notes during the interview so that you don't forget key points
- record the reasons why candidates were not appointed
- review the records of interviews for possible sex or marriage discrimination

Do

- structure the interview
- train interviewers, especially on the avoidance of bias
- issue written guidance to interviewers
- understand the job that the applicants are going for
- keep other information out of the interview
- standardise the evaluation forms

3.5 ACTION SUMMARY

- select on the basis of ability to do the job defined by a clear and non-discriminatory person specification
- keep records and monitor
- consult personnel experts if in doubt about the relevant legislation, guidelines and case law (and see Chapter 7)
- follow the Race Relations, Equal Opportunities, Fair Employment and IPM recruitment codes

Do

- use relevant selection methods, avoiding all hint of race or gender bias
- be clear, systematic and open in your methods of selection

- use multiple methods as they are more statistically reliable than single methods
- use trained people for interviewing and selection

But remember, Don't

- reject a woman candidate just because she is pregnant
- reject a candidate on the basis of union or non-union membership
- reject on the basis of irrelevant or spent convictions
- rely on gut feelings: they are often subjective and unreliable

3.6 LEGAL SUMMARY

Disabled Persons Employment Act 1944 and 1958 and (NI) Acts 1945 and 1960
For employers with 20 or more staff, this Act establishes a quota of 3% of employees who must be registered disabled.

Race Relations Act 1976 (does not apply in Northern Ireland)
Sex Discrimination Act 1975 and Sex Discrimination (NI) Order 1976 and amendment
Fair Employment (NI) Acts 1976 and 1989 and Fair Employment Monitoring Regulations (NI) 1989
These Acts define areas of discrimination and victimisation and set positive action measures for people of different ethnic and racial groups, women, married people, men and, in Northern Ireland, people of different religions or political persuasions.

Rehabilitation of Offenders Act 1974 and Exceptions Order 1975
Rehabilitation of Offenders (NI) Order 1978 and Exceptions Order 1979
These Acts allow offenders who have a 'spent' sentence not to declare it on an application form unless the application is for one of the exempt categories of jobs.

Trade Union and Labour Relations (Consolidation) Act 1992 makes it unlawful to discriminate against people who are or are not members of a trade union.

Dekker decision of the European Court of Justice regards employing pregnant women. For more information see Chapter 7.

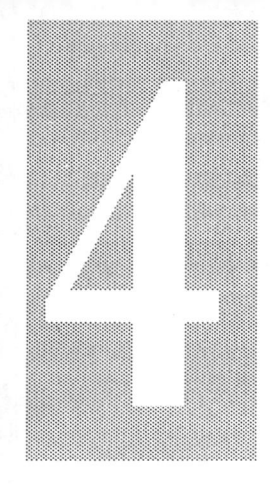

4 DECIDING ON AND APPOINTING NEW STAFF

Once you have finished the selection process, you need to decide on the best person for the job and get them into post as soon as possible.

A few places in the procedure could be tricky, so don't rush to appoint before making the necessary checks and safeguards.

KEY CONCEPTS

- references
- checks
- induction
- probation

QUESTIONS ANSWERED

- how do I reach a fair decision?
- are references useful?
- how can I get the best from a reference?
- do I need to do a medical check or a police check?
- what should I put in a rejection letter?
- what should I put in an offer letter?
- is a probationary period a good idea?
- how do I go about setting up an induction programme?

CONTENTS

1: **Reaching a decision**
Responsibility for and timing of decision on an appointment
Deciding on the best candidate
Action summary

2: **References and other checks**
References
When to take up?
Structure
Telephone references
Unsatisfactory references
Discrimination
References and confidentiality
Police checks
Medical examination
Qualification checks
Action summary

3: **Unsuccessful candidates**
Discrimination in not offering employment
Ex-offenders
Potentially suitable for another job
Action summary

4: **Offer of appointment**
The offer letter
Written terms and conditions
Action summary

5: **Induction**
Format
Induction for a person with a disability
Action summary

6: **Probation**
Action summary

7: **Action summary**

8: **Legal summary**

4.1 REACHING A DECISION

When the selection process has been completed it is good practice to make a decision immediately.

DISCRIMINATION

It is very important not to let bias creep in at the final stage.

For example:
It is not acceptable to rank an able-bodied person above a person with a disability or a non-parent above a single parent with childcare needs owing to the extra cost of meeting their needs, when they are of equal rank in all other respects.

It is unlawful not to offer a pregnant woman a job if she is the best candidate for the job, even if she is about to go on maternity leave. (See Chapter 7 for the Dekker decision, p. 274)

If a woman, man, married person, person from one of the ethnic minorities, person of a particular religion or political belief in Northern Ireland, thinks that they have been discriminated against in the selection process or in the selection decision, they can make a claim to an industrial tribunal. This claim must be made within three months of the decision.

If a tribunal finds that discrimination has occurred, it may order the company to put this right and may award damages for hurt feelings.

Responsibility for and timing of decision on an appointment

	Event or task	Responsibility	Timing
1.	Send for references	Line manager/personnel	As soon as possible
2.	Tell successful candidate informally	Chair of Panel/line manager	As soon possible
3.	Offer employment after successful references	Chair of panel/line manager	As soon possible
4.	Tell unsuccessful candidates	Chair of selection panel/line manager/personnel	Within days of interview
5.	Complete recruitment monitoring form	Line manager	As soon as possible after successful candidate accepts post

DECIDING ON THE BEST CANDIDATE

At the completion of the selection process, the selectors should rate each candidate using the score of Fully Met, Partly Met or Not Met for each criterion, based on the application form, the interview and any other selection test scores. Some interviewers use a points scoring method (for example out of 10), but this is more subjective and may lead to arguments about relative merits of different candidates. Using Fully Met, Partly Met and Not Met means you have to debate only if two candidates are very close together.

The chair should then ask each panel member to give their rating on the candidates. This should be recorded on a new specification form. The most junior member of the panel should be invited to offer opinions first, followed by second most junior, etc.

The chair adds up the number of Fully Met, Partly Met and Not Met requirements of each candidate, and informs the panel members how they compare.

Discussion on candidates can then take place. If there are candidates whose ratings are very close, then advocates of those candidates could request to re-examine the ratings on specific criteria, each putting forward their arguments. If other panel members are convinced by such arguments, which must be substantiated by evidence, then they can revise their rating. If panel members are not convinced, no change should be made. Revision of any score can only be on the grounds of error in interpreting data against criteria.

Follow the above procedure only if the rating is close; otherwise there is no need for discussion unless there is a glaring error in interpreting data against essential criteria.

If possible the decision should be made by consensus; if not, the panel should vote. If sufficient doubt arises between two candidates, see them again.

The panel should make a first and a second choice (where possible) in case the preferred candidate turns the job down or has unsatisfactory references.

The panel need to be clear about why people were not selected, and take notes of the decisions. All application forms and interview notes must be kept for 12 months after the end of the recruitment action, and monitoring forms must be kept for at least three years.

All information regarding selection is strictly confidential and must not be discussed at any point with any person other than a member of the selection panel.

The panel may decide to appoint no one. It is far better in the long run not to appoint than to appoint an unsuitable candidate. Failure to attract suitable candidates may mean that the adverts, job descriptions, application forms or person specifications were not well thought out, or that the level of pay is too low for the level of responsibility held in the job. If this happens the job will have to be readvertised.

ACTION SUMMARY

- make the decision fairly and quickly
- keep all records of interviews and decision-making
- keep candidates informed of what is happening

Do

- decide on the basis of suitability not acceptability
- stick to the answers candidates have given
- stick to clear scoring on the basis of how well the candidates meet the selection criteria
- base judgements on facts not on assumptions
- match the profile of all the job requirements against the complete profile of the individual
- concentrate on the facts revealed and the assessments made during the procedure
- pause and question whether bias has influenced the proposal to reject a candidate
- check the final decision for potential discrimination where consensus is not possible

DECIDING ON AND APPOINTING NEW STAFF

- employers with 20 or more staff should maintain a quota of registered disabled employees
- follow the rules about the employment of children and women
- employ overseas workers, except EC nationals, only after the issue of a work permit.

But remember, Don't

- be influenced either by the sexual, racial or age profile of the postholder or by any colleague's unwillingness to work with, for example, a lesbian or a black person
- listen to anecdotal evidence from staff who are involved in showing people round and who are not on the interview panel
- make any assumptions about the candidates on the basis of information not formally received
- be influenced by colleagues' stereotyping or discrimination (they may be prejudiced but there's no reason for you to be!)
- reject a person because of the nature of their disability; further advice must be taken about their disability and the availability of aids to employment or the adaptation of buildings
- allow the pregnancy of an applicant to affect the selection decision
- take criminal offences into account where they are time lapsed and where the applicant will not fall into one of the employment categories exempted by the Rehabilitation of Offenders Act

4.2 REFERENCES AND OTHER CHECKS

REFERENCES

There has been some debate recently about the value of taking up references. Is it just going through the motions when candidates inevitably give you a referee they know will be favourable? It *is* worthwhile if references are taken up in a structured fashion and questions that are specifically job related are asked.

WHEN TO TAKE UP?

A common practice is to take up references from previous employers after shortlisting but before the final interview, and to take up references for the first choice and if necessary the second choice from current employers after the interview, with the candidates' permission. This means that you have some information about all candidates before the interview, but you still have to get up-to-date information afterwards. So it may not lead to greater speed of appointment and may entail a lot of unnecessary paperwork.

If you don't want to take up references prior to interview, you can make an offer subject to satisfactory written references, but be sure to take them up properly.

STRUCTURE

When writing for a reference, structure the letter in relation to the person specification so that a specific question is asked for each criterion on the specification.

A question on the sickness record of the candidate over the past year should be asked. Also confirm that the candidate does work there in the position and on the terms they say they do, and ask about their reasons for leaving (see the sample letter on p. 134).

Do not make a blanket request for information regarding convictions. Where references mention spent or unrelated convictions they should be ignored. Employers who act on information about a spent conviction (except for jobs exempted under the Rehabilitation of Offenders Act) will be committing an unlawful act.

TELEPHONE REFERENCES

If you are in a great rush to make an offer of appointment, it can be acceptable to phone the referees, with the candidate's permission. If you do this, you should go through a structured list of questions based on what you would ask for in a written reference letter. Make sure you are speaking to the relevant person and try to talk to the line manager as opposed to a personnel person, who may not know the candidate's work very well.

Always follow up the telephone reference with a request for a written reference as well.

UNSATISFACTORY REFERENCES

If a reference is not good, the chair of the panel must investigate. Try and pin down the real reasons behind a doubtful or hesitant reference. It is possible that the referee has a grudge against the person, doesn't want them to leave or is operating in a prejudiced way.

If references are labelled 'without prejudice' or 'without legal responsibility', the writer is implying that they will take no responsibility for decisions you may make on the basis of them.

DISCRIMINATION

Don't ask questions about a black or woman candidate that you wouldn't ask about any candidate. It is unlawful to discriminate directly or indirectly in the arrangements you make for determining who should be offered employment.

REFERENCES AND CONFIDENTIALITY

If references are stored on computer then the subject has the right of access to their references by virtue of the Data Protection Act. If the reference becomes the subject of a defamation or discrimination case then the court or industrial tribunal can order it to be disclosed.

POLICE CHECKS

It may be necessary to carry out a police check on candidates for jobs that are not exempt under the Rehabilitation of Offenders Act — for example, some professions such as accountant, or people working with children (see Chapter 7).

MEDICAL EXAMINATION

In general, it is expensive to carry out medical checks on all employees. It is certainly discriminatory in intent, although not in law, to insist on blood tests for HIV.

The Institute of Personnel Management Code on Recruitment suggests that:

> the demands of most jobs require only the completion of a general health questionnaire. All information on health questionnaires must be regarded as confidential.

> *Where jobs require confirmation of specific medical and or physical requirements the recruitment policy should specify the reasons for the requirements and explain the procedures to be followed and the system for feedback of the medical results to the candidate.*

However, some organisations offer medical or health insurance as a perk. In this case joiners should take a medical check for their own benefit.

In the instance of employing people with disabilities, doctors should be asked to advise on their medical condition, not whether they are suitable to perform a particular job. There are few jobs that cannot be done by people with disabilities or that cannot be redesigned so that they can be.

Employees have the right of access to all medical reports on them from their own doctor (see Chapter 7).

The IMP also recommends that 'where the job requires a medical, the recruiter should be prepared to pay the costs of the examination and any reasonable, related travel expenses'.

QUALIFICATION CHECKS

If you have specified a particular qualification in the person specification and the candidate claims to have it, then it may be worth checking the certificate. You can ask them to bring it along to the interview or enquire of the examining body or the professional association in the case of membership of professional bodies, such as the Institute of Personnel Management or the Institute of Chartered Accountants.

Sample reference letter

Date

Dear [name]

Reference for [name] of [address]

I am writing to request a written reference for [name], who has been selected (pending successful references) for the post of [job title] (job description enclosed) at . . . and has given your name as a referee.

Could you confirm that they have been working for you as . . . since. . . .

I would like you to provide a detailed reference as to how well in your view or experience they meet the criteria on the person specification included with this letter. Could you cover each criterion separately please? If you feel you cannot comment on any point, please say why, briefly.

I would also like to know how many days sick leave [name] has taken over the last year, and whether these were spread out or consecutive. Do you have any comments to make about [name]'s time-keeping generally?

If you would like to discuss any of these points please telephone me at the above number.

I would be obliged if you could give this a high priority as we cannot make the appointment until all references have been received. I enclose a stamped

DECIDING ON AND APPOINTING NEW STAFF

> addressed envelope for your reply, which will be held in strictest confidence to the selection panel.
>
> Yours sincerely,
>
> Chair of the selection panel
> [Line manager]
>
> Encs
>
> Job description
> Person specification

ACTION SUMMARY

- take up references and make other appropriate checks, after first informing the candidate that you are doing so
- proceed to make an offer and reject unsuitable candidates

Do

- be specific in your questions for references
- take up references over the phone if you must, but get written follow-up
- investigate an unsatisfactory reference
- check qualifications if they form part of the essential person specification criteria
- keep all written information and interview notes, application forms, etc. for 12 months (3 years in Northern Ireland)

But remember, Don't

- request information about previous offences where they are lapsed or irrelevant
- discriminate in asking for information on candidates
- carry out a police check unless it is necessary for the type of work

4.3 UNSUCCESSFUL CANDIDATES

Once you have accepted your first-choice candidate and they have accepted you, you need to tell the rest that they aren't getting the job. This is an area that requires some care and attention. It is always difficult to tell someone that they haven't got a job and it is polite and lessens the blow to send a more personal letter rather than a standard letter (see the sample letter on p. 139).

- don't keep more people hanging on than necessary. At the end of the interview tell candidates when and how you will let them know, and then follow that procedure
- be prepared to talk to people
- always be clear about the reasons for rejection in a letter

The IPM Code on Recruitment recommends that you 'notify unsuccessful candidates in writing and that the recruitment policy should state if feedback is provided and by whom'.

DISCRIMINATION IN NOT OFFERING EMPLOYMENT

The law is clear that where a complainant has been interviewed but not appointed and suspects discrimination then they can request that you disclose all relevant documents, including interview notes, the application forms of all candidates, rejection letters, etc. The general rule is that unlawful discrimination is not worth it in any sense. You lose out on the best candidate and run the risk of expensive and publicly damaging legal proceedings.

> **Case law**
> Noone v. North West Thames Regional Health Authority. The complainant, from Sri Lanka, applied for a post as a consultant microbiologist. She was interviewed, but not appointed. She had better qualifications, experience and publications than the appointed candidate. Her complaint of direct race discrimination was upheld. The Court of Appeal ruled that the inference of discrimination was correct because her application was stronger than that of the appointed candidate and the employer was unable to give a satisfactory reason for having rejected her after interview.

EX-OFFENDERS

If an ex-offender's application has been unsuccessful, then you need to be particularly careful about telling them why. Standard letters of rejection may reinforce the assumptions by ex-offenders with spent convictions that there is no point in disclosing information.

- the applicant should be told if they were rejected because a conviction was considered job related

- if the applicant did not handle the disclosure of their previous conviction very well, then it would be helpful for the interviewer to give feedback on this
- records should be kept of the results of interviews so that employers are able to review their selection and recruitment procedures
- details about the applicant's convictions should always be destroyed

POTENTIALLY SUITABLE FOR ANOTHER JOB

The Institute of Personnel Management recommends that, if a candidate is considered potentially suitable for another post, agreement should be obtained from the candidate before passing them on to another interview process. In Northern Ireland, considering candidates for another job is possible only where the post has been advertised.

ACTION SUMMARY

- write a sensitive letter to those candidates not successful

Do

- be very sure of the reasons why you are not giving the job to unsuccessful candidates.

But remember, Don't

- discriminate when deciding not to appoint someone
- keep them waiting unnecessarily

Sample rejection letter

Date

Dear [name]

Job Title

Thank you for coming to the interview for the post of [job title], [whenever].

The panel was impressed by . . . .

Unfortunately we are not able to offer you the job. The standard of applicants was high and there were others who fully met more of the essential person specification criteria than you did.

I am sorry to write to you with this news. If you require more information about the decision please get in touch with [line manager] on [telephone]. I can also arrange for you to have details of the decision in writing should you wish it.

I would like to wish you luck in any future job applications you may be making.

Yours sincerely,

Chair of selection panel
[line manager]

4.4 OFFER OF APPOINTMENT

THE OFFER LETTER

The contents of a letter of appointment, together with the statement of terms and conditions and any other relevant documents, custom and practice, and terms discussed at interview form part of the employment contract.

You should be careful exactly what you put in an offer letter as terms of employment and refer to other documents where necessary — for example, the contract, the staff handbook, the discipline and grievance procedure, health and safety rules.

You should add any conditions to which the offer itself is subject and a clear timescale within which the employee is expected to accept or reject the offer (see the sample offer letter on p. 143).

If the prospective employee negotiates on any terms in the offer letter and you agree, then make sure that the final version is the one signed and accepted by both parties.

The offer letter should be sent after the receipt of satisfactory written references and medical reports or police checks if necessary. If you send the letter before the above are received, then include in the letter that the offer is subject to the above being satisfactory.

WRITTEN TERMS AND CONDITIONS

Under the 1993 **TURER Act** all employees working for 8 hours or more per week who have at least one month's service are entitled to receive written terms and conditions within two months of starting work.

WRITTEN STATEMENT OF TERMS AND CONDITIONS OF EMPLOYMENT

Current employees will be entitled to ask for a revised statement of terms and conditions if it doesn't already cover the points to be included under the new Act.

Core information must be given in one single written statement called the *Principle Statement*. Slightly more information will have to be given than before. The new points are:

- where the period of employment is temporary, the period for which it is likely to continue, or, if for a fixed term, the date it is likely to end.

- the place of work, or if the employee is required or permitted to work at various places, an indication of that fact and the employer's address.

- any collective agreements which directly affect the terms and conditions of the employment, including where the employer is not a party, the person to whom they were made.

- employers of over 20 staff will have to give an itemised pay statement to all employees working over 8 hours per week.

- conditions applying to overseas workers.

- a brief description of the job [or the job title] The written statement may refer the individual worker to other reference documents for the details of sickness, injury and sick pay; pensions; discipline and grievance procedures; applicable collective agreements; notice periods.

To remind you: the previous lawful position was (EMPLOYMENT PROTECTION [CONSOLIDATION] ACT 1978) and these following terms still have to be included:-

- name of employer
- name of employee
- date when employment began
- date on which the employee's period of continuous employment began
- the rate of pay, and the pay period (hourly, weekly, monthly)
- any rules as to hours of work including normal working hours
- entitlements to holidays, including public holidays and rates of holiday pay
- rules on absence caused by sickness or injury and on sick pay
- details of pension or pension scheme and whether the employee's pension is contracted out of the state scheme
- the length of notice the employee is entitled to receive and must give
- the employee's job title

It must also include a note specifying the following:

- any disciplinary rules affecting the employee
- a person to whom the employee can apply if they are dissatisfied with any disciplinary decision

- a person to whom the employee can take any job grievance

Changes to written particulars

Any change must be notified individually and in writing as early as possible and at the latest within one month. It may refer the employee to updated reference documents.

ACTION SUMMARY

- make your offer in careful terms
- write down points rather than relying on custom and practice
- ensure all changes to terms by negotiation are written down

---

Sample Offer Letter

Date

Dear [name],

Job Title

I am writing to confirm formally that . . . would like to offer you the post of [job title], subject to the receipt of satisfactory references.

I enclose a copy of the contract of employment that operates at . . ., which you will be required to sign should you decide to take up our offer of employment.

[Fixed-term or temporary contract details should be included here]

Salary
Your initial salary will be . . . and this is increased each year by a cost of living award and length of service up to a bar at . . . .

You have to be in post for six months to qualify for the increment, which takes place on 1 April annually.

Hours
The hours of work are 9–5 Monday to Friday, with one hour for lunch, subject to flexitime rules laid out in the contract and discussion with your line manager. [Add time off in lieu or paid overtime rules]

Benefits
[Mention the points below where relevant]

> Holiday entitlement
> Pension scheme
> Car or car loan
> Travel or season ticket loan
> Professional subscriptions paid
> Access to training and paid relevant professional qualifications training
> Childcare scheme
> Any maternity or paternity leave above the statutory minimum
> Any other working arrangements that are beneficial to carers or parents

We operate a probationary period of 3 months, extendable by a further 3 months, if necessary, for all new employees. During the probationary period either party may terminate the contract by giving seven days' notice in writing. Once the probationary

> period has been completed satisfactorily you will be confirmed in post.
>
> I would be grateful if you would contact me at the office as soon as possible to confirm your acceptance of the offer. If I haven't heard from you by . . . I will assume that you are no longer interested in the post.
>
> I look forward to hearing from you.
>
> Yours sincerely,
>
>
> Chair of selection panel
> [Director or management committee chair]

4.5 INDUCTION

Once the terms of appointment have been agreed and a start date finalised, you can plan the induction period.

One of the main causes of staff turnover in the first year is a poor introduction to the organisation. Countless times you hear stories of no one to welcome the new arrival, no desk for them, no greeting, no formal introductions, no invitations to lunch. What a way to start a relationship! If they get annoyed they are labelled as trouble makers; if they don't then they get labelled as doormats.

Starting a new job should not be some form of endurance test or hidden baptism of fire, separating the 'women from the girls' or the like. When you have spent several thousand pounds on recruiting the right person then it doesn't make sense to alienate them from day one.

An organisation interested in equal opportunities management cares about its workforce and wants to enable them to fit in quickly and well to the current team and to have their views and culture accepted.

Induction can involve two aspects: the *content* of the work and the *context* of the work. Bear in mind that there is a lot to take in and people can get rapidly saturated with overload of information. Some people change employment infrequently and may have greater difficulty — for example, women returners, people coming into the workforce after time off. Set a steady pace, with easy duties and instruction being started in the first few days, working up to fully fledged employee status after three to six months (depending on the work complexity and responsibilities).

FORMAT

The best approach uses a standard format and checklist of things new employees must be told (see checklist on p. 147), combined with a focus on the actual reservations and anxieties of individual employees.

Apart from technical employment details (such as P45 forms), concentrate first on things that the employee is going to be most worried about:

- what's my line manager like?
- what are my colleagues like?
- what's the 'culture' like?
- what standards do I have to perform to?
- how long do I have to learn them in?
- who can I ask or interrupt for help?

The main point is to give an employee confidence in their new job as soon as possible.

It can be useful to assign a new worker a 'buddy' who is not their line manager, and perhaps not in their team, who looks after them in their induction period and introduces them to the people and the organisation.

Checklist of steps in an induction programme

Their desk or workstation
The line manager
Introduction to fellow workers
Personnel details — P45, home details, emergency details
Pay and benefits details
Staff facilities — canteen, parking, nursery, etc.
Terms of employment, including disciplinary rules and grievance procedures
General nature of the work to be done
Detailed job description
Relationship of post to others
Communication procedures
Staff handbook
Personnel policies
Health and safety rules
Fire exits
Departmental rules
Probationary period format and personal attainment targets
Organisation history
Follow-up

INDUCTION FOR A PERSON WITH A DISABILITY

The same content of the programme should be followed as outlined above. In addition it is good practice to carry out the following:

- ask the new employee if they need any help and what it might be
- discuss whether they want information about their disability given to other staff
- maintain confidentiality where necessary
- where appropriate make sure that supervisors and colleagues are adequately consulted and briefed on any arrangements made with the new employee
- ensure a suitable car parking space if necessary
- give a blind person the opportunity to learn the layout of the building
- arrange that reception and other appropriate staff know if a new employee has a hearing or verbal communication difficulty and may prefer messages taken in writing
- make sure employees can have somewhere private to take medication if necessary.

ACTION SUMMARY

- plan an induction programme — ensure it's appropriate for people with disabilities
- alert staff to the presence of the new employee
- elect a 'buddy' who will do the job properly

Do

- carry out induction and take it seriously
- plan it on the basis of content and context
- base it on what the employee wants to know, not on what you think they want to know

But remember, Don't

- throw people in at the deep end
- expect them to know their way around straight away

4.6 PROBATION

Probationary periods at the start of employment are governed by a set of legal principles. If you are going to use a probationary period, you must give the employee the following details:

- the purpose of the period
- standards and review periods
- the length of the probation
- notice provisions

If the employer can show that they have set standards of performance to be met and provided training and feedback, then they can dismiss those whose performance is still unsatisfactory at the end of the period.

It is important to mention in the terms of the appointment that during the probationary period either party may terminate the contract by giving seven days' notice in writing.

The following principles are good ones to follow:

- Work out a proper procedure for assessing the worker's performance and follow it (see the sample procedure on p. 151 and sample chart of probationary period meeting on p. 154).

- Give the worker adequate opportunity to comment on and challenge any aspects of the assessment.

- Where there are any problems, work out a jointly agreed programme, including training, an agreed period for implementation and a proper review period and assessment at the end of the period.

- Where a probationary period is not confirmed, confer the right of appeal. An appeal panel must not include anyone previously involved in assessing the performance of the worker, although evidence can be taken from such people as well as from the worker concerned. Trade union representation (where recognised) should be allowed at any appeal hearing.

- Make all written assessments of the worker's performance available to that worker and any appeal panel, but this information should otherwise be kept confidential.

- Keep minutes of all meetings.

Sample probationary procedure

X Company employs all new workers on condition that they satisfactorily complete a probationary period of three months, although this may be extended a further three months at the request of either the worker or the line manager.

In the case of the post of director, the probationary interviews will be carried out by the chair of the board or management committee.

At the beginning of the period the line manager and worker will discuss the job description and agree performance standards and targets to be attained at the end of a two- and a three-month period.

There will be an induction programme running alongside the probationary period.

Two months
After two months there will be a formal interview between the line manager and the worker to discuss the worker's performance and to assess whether the agreed targets have been met. Before the meeting, the line manager will be expected to prepare a report on their assessment of the performance and to discuss it with other senior management team members as necessary.

This report will be discussed at the interview and the worker can comment on the report and make any observations about the contents or any problems they have had in carrying out the work. The meeting will be minuted and both parties asked to sign the minutes as a true record.

If there are any problems, a plan of action (including a programme of relevant training) will be agreed by both parties for review after a further month. At this point the probationary period may be extended by a further month (to four months in total) if it is felt that improvements or training could not adequately be assessed within one month. This plan of action should be fully minuted.

Three or four months
A further interview with written report will be held for all probationers at the end of three months (or four months if the period has been extended), again fully minuted. Where there have been no problems, the worker is confirmed in post.

If a serious problem (for example, poor timekeeping) becomes apparent before the end of the two-month period, then this should be addressed immediately, and not at the end of the period.

Where there have been problems, the plan of training and improvements is reviewed with comments from the worker. The worker is told whether their appointment is to be confirmed or the probationary period to be extended for a further period (up to six months in total).

Where the probationary period is to be extended, a further review must be held at the end of the six-month period to discuss the worker's performance. At the end of this period the worker will be formally confirmed in post or not.

Appeal
The worker may appeal against a negative decision within three working days of the receipt of the formal letter of non-confirmation to the [most relevant person] next senior line manager, personnel manager, regional manager or chair of the management

DECIDING ON AND APPOINTING NEW STAFF

> committee and may have a trade union representative present at any appeal hearing.
>
> The relevant person must convene an appeal hearing within 10 working days of the receipt of the complaint. This will normally consist of . . . and a line manager who is not the probationer's manager.
>
> The appeal committee will take notice of the minutes of all review meetings and will interview the line manager concerned and the probationer before reaching a decision. The decision of the appeal panel is final.
>
> No one gets more than two reviews [one ideally, two in exceptional circumstances].

EQUAL OPPORTUNITIES

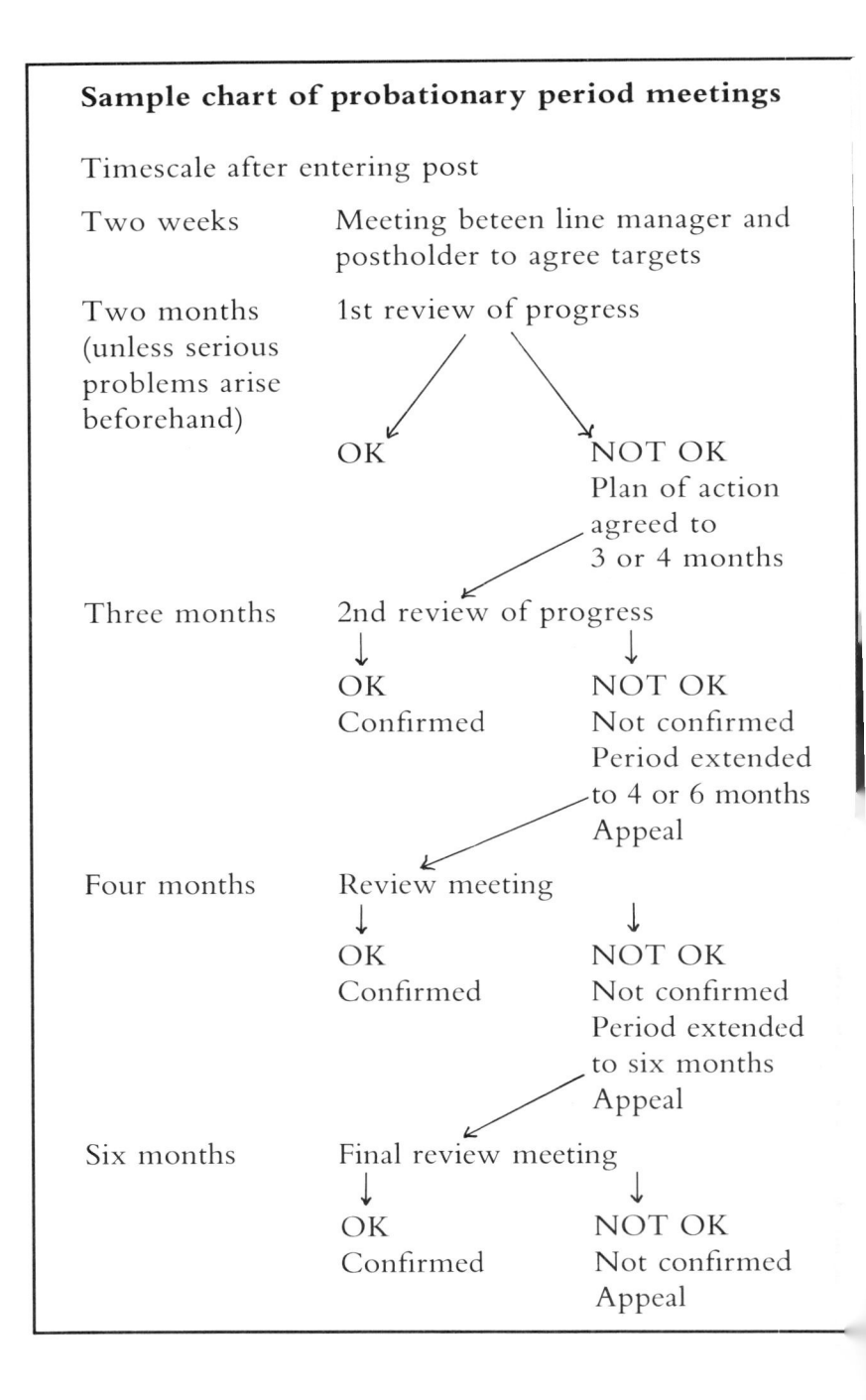

Sample chart of probationary period meetings

Timescale after entering post

Two weeks	Meeting beteen line manager and postholder to agree targets
Two months (unless serious problems arise beforehand)	1st review of progress

                                        OK   NOT OK
                                                                     Plan of action agreed to 3 or 4 months

Three months	2nd review of progress	
	OK Confirmed	NOT OK Not confirmed Period extended to 4 or 6 months Appeal
Four months	Review meeting	
	OK Confirmed	NOT OK Not confirmed Period extended to six months Appeal
Six months	Final review meeting	
	OK Confirmed	NOT OK Not confirmed Appeal

Sample letter: Confirmed in post

Date

Dear [name]

Probationary period

After the meeting we had to review your progress in the post, I discussed this with the director.

I would like to confirm that we consider your probationary period is now over and that you are to be fully confirmed in the post of [job title].

I would also like to take this opportunity to say [something complimentary, e.g. how well you have fitted in to the staff team, etc.].

Yours sincerely,

Line manager

> **Sample letter: Not confirmed in post**
>
> Date
>
> Dear [name]
>
> **Probationary period**
>
> Further to our meeting yesterday, and after discussions with the director, I am afraid that we are of the opinion that not enough progress has been made on meeting the targets set in the final meeting of the probationary review period.
>
> In view of . . . [reason for decision], I am sorry to tell you that . . . Company do not feel able to confirm you in the post of [job title]. You are therefore given notice to leave your post one week from today [date].
>
> Yours sincerely,
>
> Line manager

ACTION SUMMARY

- if you're going to use a probationary period, plan it properly
- manage the performance of workers particularly closely over the period to be fair to them and you

Do

- be clear with yourself and the employees about any probationary period
- work out a proper programme for assessing performance
- give the worker an opportunity to comment on and challenge any aspects of their assessment
- give the right of appeal

4.7 ACTION SUMMARY

- decide on the best candidate fairly
- make all necessary checks and references
- follow the legal requirements carefully when writing an offer letter
- devise a sensitive induction programme and get someone to 'buddy' the new worker
- set up a probationary period with proper standards and targets
- keep all the results of interviews and decision-making for 12 months (three years in Northern Ireland)
- feed back the results to the person monitoring equal opportunities

4.8 LEGAL SUMMARY

REFERENCES

There is no legal obligation to provide a reference. However, if they are given then employers owe a duty to potential employers to provide *true and accurate references* and not to be negligent or misleading by any omissions. A recent court of appeal decision held that, as a general proposition, a referee holds no duty of care to the subject of the reference. That is, you can give a bad reference if it is still honest and does not defame the person concerned.

MEDICAL RECORDS

The **Access to Medical Reports Act 1988** allows a person to have access to a medical report about them if it is prepared by their own doctor
The **Access to Medical Records Act 1990**, however, allows an individual access to medical *records* held by any medical practitioner (their own or a company doctor or specialist).

EX-OFFENDERS

Rehabilitation of Offenders Act 1974 and Exemptions Order 1975
Rehabilitation of Offenders (NI) Order 1978 and Exceptions Order 1979
These Acts specify when an employee has to declare a previous conviction on application forms.

DATA PROTECTION

If you keep references on computer, then employees have a right of access to them under the **Data Protection Act 1984.**

DISCRIMINATION

Race Relations Act 1976, section 4(1), and **Sex Discrimination Act 1975**, section 6(1)
An employer may not discriminate directly or indirectly against women, men, married people or people from different racial or ethnic groups:

(a) in the arrangements made for determining who should be offered employment

(b) in the terms on which employment is offered

(c) by refusing or deliberately omitting to offer employment

The **Dekker judgment, European Court of Justice**, means that you must not discriminate against pregnant women in offers of employment, just because of their pregnancy.

RELIGIOUS BELIEF OR POLITICAL OPINION (NORTHERN IRELAND)

Fair Employment (NI) Acts 1976 and 1989 and **Fair Employment Monitoring Regulations (NI) 1989** (do not apply in Great Britain).
The purpose of these Acts is to ensure equality of opportunity in employment in Northern Ireland, irrespective of religious belief or political opinion.

TERMS AND CONDITIONS

Trade Union Reform and Employment Rights (TURER) Act 1993

All new employees working for more than 8 hours per week who have at least one month's service will be entitled to receive written terms and conditions within two months of starting work (previously 13 weeks).

The Contracts of Employment and Redundancy Payments Act (NI) as amended 1965 specifies similar terms and conditions of employment for Northern Ireland.

Under the terms of the **Employment Act 1990**, an employer who makes a spurious offer of employment (defined as an offer that no employer who wanted to fill the post would make) may be subject to litigation.

The **Trade Union Consolidation Act 1992** makes it unlawful to make an offer subject to membership or non-membership of a trade union.

5 EMPLOYMENT

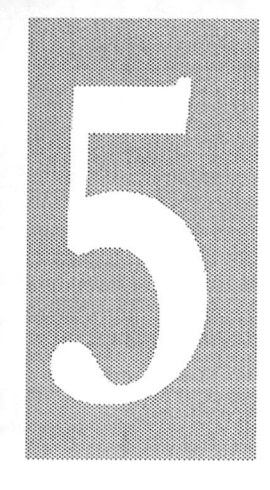

Access to equal opportunities in employment differs for different groups of employees. The effects of discrimination faced by lesbians and gay men will be different from those faced by women, black people and other ethnic minorities, or people with disabilities. Types of discrimination and experience of it will vary within groups of people: some may never face overt harassment, some may come up against problems all the time. This chapter covers *employment* issues rather than *management* issues for people at work. Management issues will be dealt with in other Industrial Society publications.

KEY CONCEPTS

- staff development
- harassment
- grievance procedures
- disciplinary procedures

QUESTIONS ANSWERED

- what is good practice to offer in terms and conditions of employment?
- how do I organise a staff development programme?
- what are the rules governing promotion and equal opportunities?
- what is positive action training?
- can I dismiss someone straight away for harassment?
- what needs to go into a disciplinary and grievance policy?

CONTENTS

1: Contractual issues
Issues for different groups of employees
    Lesbians and gay men
    Black and ethnic minority people
    Women
    Part-time workers
    Working people with children or other caring responsibilities
    People who are HIV+ or have AIDS
    People with disabilities
Contract terms and conditions
Pay
Maternity pay
Sickness pay
Leave
Access to benefits
Action Summary

2: Staff Development
Support, supervision and appraisal
Training and continuous development
    Access to training for staff
    Coaching
    Mentoring
    Training and career development for women, black and ethnic minority staff
    Women-only and black and ethnic minority only courses
    Training under positive action provisions
    Career development
Promotions, transfers, regrading, redeployments
    Barriers to promotion
    Codes of practice
Action Summary

3: **Harassment**
   What is harassment?
   But it doesn't happen here!
   Developing a policy on harassment
   Action in cases of harassment
     Employee
     Employers
   Procedures
     Informal stage
     Formal stage
     Counselling
     Grievance and disciplinary panel
     Disciplinary action
   Action Summary
4: **Disciplinary, grievance and dismissal procedures**
   General guidelines
   Grievance procedures
   Disciplinary procedures
   Dismissal
     Pregnancy dismissal
     Fair dismissal
     Summary dismissal
   Appeal procedures
   Action Summary
5: **Action summary**
6: **Legal summary**

5.1 CONTRACTUAL ISSUES

Addressing equality issues through the contract is an important way of ensuring that all employees have access to the same terms and conditions, benefits and sanctions. As well as changing the contract, you will need to ensure that the equal opportunities policy states that the organisation will be tackling discrimination in employment for all workers.

Some of the main points of terms and conditions that are most relevant for equal opportunities implementation are:

- facilitating job-sharing and part-time working
- flexitime
- paternity or co-parenting leave
- carer's responsibilities
- ability to take holidays at times other than Christian festivals
- ability for workers to work over Christian festivals where appropriate
- provision for long holidays to be taken to visit relatives abroad
- recognition that people other than those who are married may have responsibility for partners, children and other dependants
- good provision for parental responsibility leave
- regulations about who can have pensions and other fringe benefits
- access to sick pay and leave
- access to compassionate leave

Improving these factors creates an environment that enables people to work more productively. By being aware of how people choose to live their lives, the contract of employment can be a help not a hindrance.

ISSUES FOR DIFFERENT GROUP OF EMPLOYEES

LESBIANS AND GAY MEN

Lesbians and gay men have been continuously discriminated against in employment on the grounds of their sexuality. In many instances this has led to unfair dismissal. More often, workers are passed over for promotion or simply asked to resign once it is known they are lesbian or gay. Teachers, social workers, nursery workers and housing residential workers have been particularly vulnerable to victimisation.

At present an additional factor that operates to increase prejudice against lesbians and gay men is fear of AIDS. Most people are either uninformed or misinformed about AIDS and what is involved in being HIV positive or how AIDS is transmitted.

Lesbian and gay people have no rights under the law to protection against discrimination and victimisation on the grounds of their sexuality, although the EC is considering this as a proposal in the near future. Changes in employment practices and conditions of service are the most positive way that organisations can challenge discrimination and promote policies on equality of opportunity for lesbians and gay men.

Changes in employment practice should be made regardless of whether there are any lesbians or gay men who are open about their sexuality in the workplace. By securing the rights of lesbians and gay men you can create the kind of working environment where they can be open if they wish.

BLACK AND ETHNIC MINORITY PEOPLE

By the mid 1970s two out of every five black and ethnic minority people in Britain were born here. There are at least 2 million black and ethnic minority British people who face severe discrimination in access to employment, housing, education and public services.

In employment, black and ethnic minority people tend to be concentrated in the lower job levels in a way that cannot be explained by lower academic or job qualifications. They tend to do more shift work, but shift work premiums do not raise their earnings levels because the jobs are intrinsically badly paid.

A Policy Studies Institute survey in 1990 found that the level of unemployment among black and ethnic minority people was higher than that of white people — 15.1% among Afro-Caribbean men, 9.9% among Asian men and only 6.9% for white men. Young West Indian men and all black and ethnic minority women experienced the highest unemployment rates.

Once unemployed, black and ethnic minority people tend to stay unemployed for longer. The percentage of black and ethnic minority women who are long-term unemployed is twice that of white women.

Racism in Britain is subtle as well as overt and runs through all aspects of society. No organisation can consider itself free from racist assumptions and practices; this includes the voluntary sector and community organisations. Action needs to be taken to redress the discrimination. This action needs to be central to the organisations concerned and a conscious long-term strategy. Workers, managers, management committee and board members need to examine assumptions, change strategies, take positive initiatives and make committed choices about where to place the organisation's resources.

WOMEN

Sexism operates throughout society. It affects all women in all aspects of their lives through prescribing the roles and behaviour that are acceptable. This in turn affects women's access to housing, jobs, earnings, education and political clout. A strong women's movement has made a difference to women's lives, but much more remains to be challenged before we begin to approach equality.

Women and men participate in the marketplace on very different terms. Women are concentrated in a smaller number of occupations than men, mostly in the low-paid service industries. Women's average hourly earnings are still only 79% of men's, despite the Equal Pay legislation. Black women face even greater discrimination: they are found in the very lowest-paid and least secure sectors of the workforce. Lesbian women continue to face insecurity at work and fear of losing their jobs if they are open about who they are.

The shape of many women's working lives is determined by caring responsibilities. Women constitute 90% of all part-time workers, and the jobs are usually worse paid and with poorer terms and conditions. The government refuses to accept responsibility for improving state childcare provision in spite of recent evidence that the economy needs trained, skilled workers to stay in the workforce. It prefers to leave incentives to individual firms rather than change its attitude to women as workers: a flexible, cheap labour force to be called on in times of crisis.

PART-TIME WORKERS

There are many ways in which part-time workers can lose out on benefits at work. A DE/OPCS survey of women and employment found that 28% of part-timers were excluded from all of the following: sick pay, pensions, training and promotion, compared with only 8% of full-timers.

WORKING PEOPLE WITH CHILDREN OR OTHER CARING RESPONSIBILITIES

Although it is still mainly women who look after children or other dependants, this often reflects society's prohibitions rather than their choice. Organisations need to provide terms and conditions that are beneficial to all people with childcare and other caring responsibilities.

It is important to recognise that people with parental or other caring responsibilities need time off to deal with those responsibilities (such as a child's illness) and not to have to take sick leave or annual leave in order to do it.

Employers should adopt leave provisions that cover not just the traditional maternity leave, but also paternity leave and shared responsibility leave. This benefits lesbian and gay people in partnerships with children where shared parenting operates and also helps people who are taking on childcare responsibilities where they are not a biological parent.

PEOPLE WHO ARE HIV+ OR HAVE AIDS

All workplaces should adopt health and safety guidelines and take steps to challenge misinformation and any resulting prejudice that may arise.

PEOPLE WITH DISABILITIES

Unemployment rates for people with disabilities are at least twice those of people without disabilities, and may be more as official figures count only people who are registered disabled.

The special contractual issues for people with disabilities are: other people's attitudes, consultation and workplace adaptations.

Attitudes Other people's expectations or fears are often the biggest obstacle for people with disabilities. As a manager your job is to consult with the individual to find out what they need to facilitate their work and how much information about their disability they wish to share with colleagues.

They should also be able to feel free to come to you with any problems or lack of understanding they encounter from other staff.

Consultation It is imperative to consult the person about their needs. They know their disability intimately and can often suggest the easiest solutions to their needs.

For example:
When Helen needed to use a wheelchair at work they were planning to ramp the whole front entrance. She pointed out that the back entrance was already ramped and had a convenient nearby parking space. She just needed authorisation to use it!

Adaptations Whether you are recruiting a new employee or retaining an employee who has become disabled while working with you, many aids, adaptations and financial grants are available to enable that employee to work effectively.

Some employees don't need work aids.

For example:
Alison Cornfield is blind and works as an audiotypist. She uses the standard equipment provided in the typing pool and the supervisor finds her work excellent.

Sue Gregory has diabetes and needs to inject herself regularly. She does not need any workplace adaptations, merely somewhere private to attend to her medical needs.

Normal modern office equipment and furniture are often of a high enough standard to enable people with disabilities to work effectively. If all your chairs are ergonomically designed, then everyone will benefit, not just people who already have a disability!

Simple rearrangements of the workplace might help other workers with disabilities.

For example:
Geoffrey has a hearing impairment that makes it very hard for him to work with background noise. His desk has been moved to be in the furthest corner of the office away from the switchboard.

Code of Good Practice The Employment Service has published a Code of Good Practice on the Employment of Disabled People. This covers:

1. Deciding on a policy — a section for senior managers
2. Putting the policy into practice, advice to managers
3. Descriptions of disablement
4. An examination of common concerns of employers in recruitment of people with disabilities
5. The recruitment and selection process
6. People with disabilities at work
7. Assisting employees who become disabled
8. The role of employees and their representatives
9. Co-ordination of policy and practice
10. Help with drawing up a policy
11. Sources of practical and financial help and advice

Grants to employers of people with disabilities From April 1994 there will be a new unified scheme of help called 'Access to Work'. This will incorporate existing provision but will make some adjustments too. Employers will have to make a 50% contribution towards the cost of special equipment costing up to £100. New help will include:

- communication support for deaf people in the workplace

- personal support for people with learning difficulties or severe physical difficulties

- personal support to help people with mental health problems settle in to a job

- adaptations to vehicles

CONTRACT TERMS AND CONDITIONS

PAY

Equal pay for work of equal value is a statutory right within any organisation under the **Equal Pay Act.** The rules and regulations governing this right are complex, so if you need further information consult the personnel department or legal department.

MATERNITY PAY

By October 1994 the rules on maternity pay will have changed from the current system to comply with the EC Pregnant Workers Directive. Ensure that you are operating a fair system that doesn't discriminate against part-timers or other staff. Try to offer better than statutory rights.

SICKNESS PAY

Part-time staff should receive full sick leave entitlement, but sick pay should be reduced pro rata. Owing to Statutory Sick Pay (SSP) rules, some part-time staff may not be eligible for SSP either because they are not sick for long enough to qualify or because they do not earn enough to meet the minimum earnings requirement for SSP. It is important therefore that organisations should include all staff, especially part-time staff, in any sick pay scheme or health insurance scheme that they are part of. Guaranteed income during periods of sickness is as crucial to part-timers as it is to full-timers.

LEAVE

Annual Leave If annual leave entitlement accrues with seniority rather than length of service, then this indirectly discriminates against women, as far fewer women are employed at senior levels. Entitlement to more annual leave should depend on length of service where this is applicable. However, many men often have longer service than women so this also may have a discriminatory effect.

Leave arrangements Adopt a leave policy that allows for extended leave arrangements and also has flexibility for:

- employment breaks
- emergency leave
- discretionary leave

Leave arrangements for those who wish to take leave at other than Christian festivals should be facilitated. For example, an entitlement to a certain number of days holiday per year should be additional to statutory holidays.

> **Case law**
> Seventeen Asian-origin textile workers were awarded damages after receiving a final warning over taking unauthorised time off. A decision from the Leeds industrial tribunal ruled that the firm should have taken measures to allow the men time off to celebrate EID, the main festival of the muslim year, especially as they had offered to work extra hours to compensate.

Paternity leave Paternity leave should be extended to all workers and be increased to a reasonable level. People other than the biological father should be able to apply if they are acting as a co-parent for either a new baby or adoption purposes.

Compassionate leave This clause in the contract should be extended to cover cohabitants, lovers and close friends, and may need to define what the organisation would consider to be a close friend.

Carer's responsibility leave Looking after sick children, caring for sick dependants or dealing with a breakdown in normal childcare arrangements often fall on women in a partnership. Workers often have to take sick leave or annual leave or apply for special compassionate leave to deal with domestic crises or illnesses. Carers need access to leave as a right to deal with such emergencies.

Examples of provision vary from 5 to 20 days a year. The majority allow for paid time off at the discretion of senior management for periods longer than the minimum. Where this is the case, then the decision-making needs to be swift so that workers are not in any doubt as to their rights and their colleagues can be informed.

Leave during school holidays Arrangements can often be difficult during the school holidays for those with young children. Organisations could consider making a leave provision for parents to take extra time off during school holidays, to work at home, or to vary their hours at these times.

ACCESS TO BENEFITS

Paid benefits Confirm that employees can nominate persons other than spouses as the beneficiaries of health or pensions insurance policies taken out in the workplace.

Pensions and life assurance schemes A recent study by the EOC showed that women are discriminated against in the type and level of benefits in employers' pensions and life assurance schemes. Organisations should look at their schemes to ensure that they are relevant and equal. This is particularly important for part-time workers, who are unlikely to take out this sort of cover themselves.

Working from home It can help people with childcare responsibilities to be able to work at home for some periods of time. Organisations could consider this as an alternative arrangement where workers request it and it is feasible.

Childcare and carers' costs If organisations require people with parental responsibilities to work outside their normal working hours, then they should offer childcare or other caring costs for any alternative arrangements that have to be made.

Childcare/carers' subsidy Some organisations have recognised that, as a part of their commitment to equal opportunities, it is important to offer childcare subsidies to allow parents, and particularly women, better access to career development. With the aid of the subsidy employees can make better arrangements for care and can thus make a better, more relaxed contribution in the workplace.

ACTION SUMMARY

- ensure you are offering anti-discriminatory terms and conditions, especially for:
    - part-time workers
    - pensions schemes
    - maternity leave, carer's leave and compassionate leave
- consider developing contractual options on, for example:
    - paternity and co-parent leave
    - parental responsibility leave
    - carers' leave
    - childcare and carers' costs
    - childcare and caring subsidy

But remember, Don't

- deliberately offer worse rights to part-timers or to women

5.2 STAFF DEVELOPMENT

People who traditionally face discrimination are underrepresented in the workforce at every level, but particularly at senior levels. Each organisation must consider the barriers to the development of the potential of all its staff in access to training, promotion and routes to success. Such blocks will almost inevitably involve discrimination, prejudice and stereotyping of one sort or another. A clear policy on staff development is therefore a prerequisite of an equal opportunities management approach.

For example:
Gerry is a middle manager in a wholesale fruit distribution network. He has always made life difficult for his female subordinates, never sending them on training or recommending them for promotion. They complain sometimes to the personnel officer, but more often leave as soon as possible. Instead of tackling Gerry about this problem, the senior staff have decided to wait another four years and then offer him early retirement. Who loses most?

Apart from the fact that it is unlawful under the Sex Discrimination Act and Race Relations Act to discriminate in selection for training and promotion or in access to benefits, the organisation will be under-utilising skills and talents.

SUPPORT, SUPERVISION AND APPRAISAL

SUPPORT

All workers need to feel that their contribution is valued and their opinions heard, to have positive feedback on their work and to work in an environment free from discrimination. There are various ways in which people find these in work: through formal supervision sessions, through team work and through informal and formal group support.

In some instances, however, the support that is available may not be adequate. For example, workers who are the only black, lesbian, gay or woman worker may be isolated at work and facing discrimination that they cannot stomach challenging every time as the lone voice.

Different workers have different needs for support inside and outside of work. It is up to managers not to be judgemental but to offer every means available to support the worker. Where this is not possible or satisfactory as direct support, then time and resources must be made available for workers to support each other or to seek support outside the workplace, for example in women's groups or black workers' groups.

People may feel the need for support differently at different times. If the space is there and the recognition that it is legitimate to take advantage of it, then workers can use it as appropriate in response to the work situation.

Internally, workers can show support for colleagues by taking on demands raised and bringing them to the wider staff group by giving value to the individual's work, by listening to their experience and learning from it, and by accepting that another's experience is valid and not trying to reduce it to fit in with one's own experience.

SUPERVISION AND APPRAISAL

An appraisal system that is perceived as supportive and development for employees as well as providing the opportunity for checking competencies and performance standards is one way in which staff can be more formally supported in their work.

The extension of that is to give proper time and energy to supervision within the framework of appraisal. This is a crucial aspect of its success and also provides a great opportunity to assess learning needs.

TRAINING AND CONTINUOUS DEVELOPMENT

The IPM Code on Continuous Development recommends that:

Self-development, team learning and continuous organisational development all require resource material and facilities. The organisation should have clear policies and practice on the following:

> *Training and learning budgets*
> *Authorisation of training and learning plans*
> *Facilities and support for study during and outside working hours, including paid and unpaid leave*
> *Open and distance learning*
> *Financial assistance with courses, travel, books, tapes, and other facilities*
> *Awards or scholarships*
> *Access to internal advisers, counsellors and developers*
> *Coaching and tutorial resources*

All employees should be made aware of the policy and range of facilities and opportunities for learning that are available.

ACCESS TO TRAINING FOR STAFF

Training plays a key part in employees' job performance and career development and may also affect their success in internal promotion, transfer and regrading. Training opportunities must be made available to all workers, whether on internal training or access to external courses. A distinction should be made between training to improve job performance and training to acquire new skills. Where appropriate, the links should be made plain between acquiring new skills and the possibilities for regrading within the organisation, so that all workers understand their options and are encouraged to take advantage of opportunities.

Training should be made available to those traditionally discriminated against in access to skills and opportunities in a fair proportion. Take-up of training courses should be monitored.

Where career development schemes and training courses for new managers are offered in the organisation, there should be fair access to these courses for all staff. Take-up of opportunities should be monitored to ensure this fair access is taking place.

> **Case law**
> Bath v. Bedfordshire County Council 1993. An Asian ethnic minority specialist careers officer who was not selected for a training course that would enable him to carry out his duties was discriminated against on the grounds of race. It found that the interviews were a sham and awarded £1,000 compensation.

COACHING

Coaching is a form of on-the-job training using work to provide planned opportunities for learning under guidance. It assists individuals to think through their problems and develop appropriate solutions. It is a very powerful training tool because this process requires the learner to evaluate options, solve problems and plan actions. As the learning takes place on the job it fulfils a lot of the criteria for successful learning.

The coaching process consists of three overlapping parts: learning, problem solving, and planning. The typical process for coaching is as follows:

1. coach and worker agree to start coaching and agree a time and place

2. the length of each session is agreed

3. both parties consider the purpose of the session beforehand

4. the agenda for the session is agreed and worked on

The difference between coaching and other forms of support and supervision is that the coach seeks to improve skills, knowledge and attitudes in dealing with the particular situation being worked on. This will happen through analysis of the situation, identifying objectives for a suitable solution, listing and examining options, developing the best action plan, implementing this and reviewing the outcome. The review is not just about outcomes, but about the processes the worker uses in completing the action plan or tasks involved. This level of review encourages the worker to identify the level of learning that has occurred and how this might be used in other situations.

The crucial element of the coaching process is that the manager must be available for discussion and assistance as required, but, having set up the plan, must encourage learning and discovery through the completion of the plan and the review, not by taking over part way through — unless there are unseen dangers.

Coaching is useful where the skills, knowledge and attitudes being developed are in areas where the learner must make decisions and where there might be no absolute or correct way.

The skills, knowledge and attitudes of a good coach are:

Skills: good listener, appropriate use of questions, good communicator, good planner and good problem-solving skills;
Knowledge: understanding of how people learn, some knowledge of the situation being worked on, non-verbal communication messages;
Attitudes: awareness of people's needs, equal opportunities issues and development needs.

MENTORING

Mentoring is a similar process to coaching but with more emphasis on career development and support through the organisation's hierarchy. Mentoring is perhaps able to offer a wider range of support for the protege, with coaching being one element of it. The mentor is more likely to be a senior manager than an immediate line manager and perhaps from a different department. They could be of the same race or sex as the protege to enhance the sense of identifying with the mentor.

The difficulties of mentoring may be mismatch of individuals, unreal expectations on both sides and the time and effort involved.

TRAINING AND CAREER DEVELOPMENT FOR WOMEN, BLACK AND ETHNIC MINORITY STAFF

Black and ethnic minority people and women in particular tend to be employed in the lowest-grade positions and to get stuck in low-paid jobs. The organisation can adopt positive training policies for both internal training and attendance on external courses, which should be advertised among women and black and ethnic minority staff.

Any courses that lead to possibilities for regrading among staff should be explained to black and ethnic minority staff and they should be encouraged to attend. Sessions with supervisors should include discussions on options for promotion and career development within the organisation.

WOMEN-ONLY AND BLACK AND ETHNIC MINORITY ONLY COURSES

Research has shown that people who face discrimination in employment and access to higher levels in hierarchies do better when they go on courses that are intended for particular groups alone — for example, women-only courses. Organisations should consider providing such training or finding external courses for their staff to attend.

TRAINING UNDER POSITIVE ACTION PROVISIONS

The Race Relations Act, section 35, makes explicit the lawfulness of offering facilities and service provision to meet the special needs of racial groups in regard to their education, training and welfare or any ancillary benefits.

Section 37 (Sex Discrimination Act, section 47) makes it lawful in certain cases for a training body to offer special training for racial groups not represented or underrepresented in identified trades, professions, etc., while section 38 (SDA, s48) allows employers to make training provision for staff of racial groups (or women) not represented or underrepresented in all parts of the workforce and to encourage them to apply for posts where they have been underrepresented in the past 12 months.

It is worth considering these options if your organisation is large enough.

CAREER DEVELOPMENT

People facing discrimination in employment often find themselves stuck in dead-end jobs, despite any qualifications they may have. The changes outlined above should go some way to redressing this. However, it is also important to discuss career plans with workers and to facilitate their development in the job and their access to promotion within the organisation.

Secretarial and administrative staff (who are also more likely to work part time) are in jobs that may make it difficult for them to develop into policy or managerial areas. They need access not only to fair terms and conditions of employment, but also to equal pay and regrading through non-discriminatory job evaluation schemes. They should be targeted for skills training and career planning sessions and given access to on-the-job training schemes, external training or day-release courses. Larger organisations can examine their career structure and institute supportive career development plans for secretarial and administrative staff.

PROMOTIONS, TRANSFERS, REGRADING, REDEPLOYMENTS

Organisations that are large enough need a policy on internal promotions and transfers.

Internal appointment tends to reinforce the status quo as regards the racial and sexual composition of the workforce and is therefore not a fair policy in all situations. Potentially, however, internal appointment can offer employment opportunities for those within the organisation who are stuck in low-paid, low-status jobs. The success of this depends upon there being training and career development opportunities for those workers; and is dependent on there being a greater representation of black and women workers in the lower-paid jobs than in the rest of the organisation.

All regradings should be open to women, black people and ethnic minorities, lesbians, gays and people with disabilities. Performance should be monitored as part of the employment monitoring process. The operation of regrading should be tied into internal training schemes and job evaluation schemes that have been examined for bias or discriminatory content and structure. All people need to know that they can apply for regrading, rather than having to wait for the organisational mechanisms to take their course.

> **Case law**
> Riches v. Express Dairy 1992. A female candidate was asked a series of questions about her childcare responsibilities when applying for promotion to a supervisor role. The tribunal concluded that a man would not have been cross-examined in such a way, and noted that the questions were entirely contrary to the EOC Code of Practice.

BARRIERS TO PROMOTION

The barriers to promotion are the same as the barriers to employment in the first place:

- inappropriate access to application
- unfair or inappropriate selection criteria that rule out certain people
- discrimination by the selectors

Direct discrimination occurs when workers or managers say, 'We don't want a woman boss' or 'The clients wouldn't like a black senior supervisor'. This precludes women and black people even applying or being put forward for promotion.

Even when they do get to the promotion panel, discriminatory and stereotyped attitudes of the selectors may operate against them.

Structural

Ladders. Where there is one point of entry — for women, say, this is to the typing pool and then to becoming a personal assistant — there may be few opportunities to break into supervision or management.

Informal procedures and lack of openness about promotion criteria can allow stereotyped ideas to continue unchecked — for example, that managers need aggressive, competitive and ambitious natures and that men have those qualities but women do not, or that Asian people are passive and therefore don't make good managers.

Case law

Mann v. Moody and others. An administrative assistant of Asian origin in the Department of Social Security was discriminated against by a senior officer when he assessed her application for promotion. The senior officer had commented favourably on her performance as an administrative assistant but then said that he encountered a mental reservation about Miss Mann that would not have been present if she were a white person. He made stereotyped assumptions that because she is of Asian origin and because she is softly spoken, she lacked drive and would not be acceptable to white subordinates.

Appointment and promotion depending on friendship or contact networks are also discriminatory.

Unrealistic or discriminatory criteria include: educational or training qualifications set too high; British qualifications only specified; length of service specified; continuity of service rated higher than careers with breaks.

An inflexible or hostile work environment is one in which working arrangements are inflexible; long hours are demanded; colleagues are intimidating; subordinates are not discouraged from racism or sexism, homophobia or other overtly hostile actions.

Setting the person up to fail means putting all the barriers in the way and then saying it is their own fault they failed, or demanding higher standards from women, black or gay managers.

Past discrimination in education or training can lead to it being impossible to catch up unless criteria for successful performance on the job, positive action training or training at work are emphasised as more important.

CODES OF PRACTICE

The Codes of Practice from the EOC, CRE and FEC recommend the following:

- operate promotion practices so as to ensure the appointment of the best person for the job
- organise selection for promotion and transfers along the same lines as recruitment — exercise special care where there are age limits, mobility requirements or seniority lists in operation
- consider whether the job could be shared or held by two part-time workers

- publicise all vacancies to internal as well as external candidates
- ensure the procedures for promotion are in writing and available to all staff
- state who is designated to approve appointments and to take part in the selection process
- assess all possible candidates — do not use discriminatory assessment criteria
- monitor each stage of the process
- do not assume that proven ability at a lower level necessarily implies a good prospect of success higher up the ladder
- where an appraisal system is in operation, assessment criteria should be examined to ensure that they are not unlawfully discriminatory — for example, length of service is a criterion that may be unlawful

ACTION SUMMARY

- assess problem areas in the company where different groups are underrepresented at senior levels or in access to career development
- adopt a company-wide continuous development, staff development or career development programme for all employees, set targets and monitor it to make sure discrimination is not still operating

- develop a corporate strategy involving:
  - support, supervision, appraisal, and the identification of learning and training needs
  - in-house training, external training, learning on the job, mentoring, coaching, continuous development
  - a clear policy and priorities on access to resources for training
  - consideration of the need for positive action training
- develop accelerated development and training schemes for women and black staff if they are underrepresented
- encourage line managers to urge underrepresented groups to take advantage of company opportunities for training and development, throughout the staff development policy
- review your practice on promotion, regrading, transfers and redeployment
- publish policies and make them clear to all staff and line managers
- train the selectors for promotion panels in the same way as you would for selection panels and operate the same safeguards in the interview process
- monitor the results

But remember, Don't

- make stereotyped assumptions about people's motivations at different staff grades, across one sex or race of employee
- ask about their circumstances
- rule people out for spurious reasons

5.3 HARASSMENT

Where behaviour on the part of a worker, manager, volunteer, client, customer or user is racist, sexist, anti-lesbian, anti-gay, against people with disabilities, or clearly discriminatory in some other fashion, then firm action must be taken straight away.

WHAT IS HARASSMENT?

Harassment represents a range of behaviour that is unwanted, uninvited and often repeated, and intrudes into people's lives. It is an expression of power or domination over one group of people by another because they are perceived to be a threat to the dominant group's existence or power.

Harassment can take a variety of forms, from a violently abusive attack to the 'dripping tap' accumulation of intrusions. For example, most sexual harassment involves men who think that they have the right to demand time and attention from women and will invoke that right whenever they choose. Or harassment may involve patronising statements. Or people may be ignored, left out of the process of consultation at work and treated differently from the other workers in a subtle manner.

The difficulty of defining and categorising harassment is precisely what deters people from reporting it or complaining of behaviour that causes distress. They run the risk of not being believed, of having their experiences trivialised or of being accused of 'provoking' it. They may also fear retribution or embarrassment.

No one invites or provokes harassment. It is a contradiction in terms to suggest that people deliberately invite insulting behaviour.

BUT IT DOESN'T HAPPEN HERE!

But it does! Some evidence on sexual harassment in the workplace is as follows:

- NALGO in London found that 7 out of 10 women had faced sexual harassment at work
- Alfred Marks Bureau found that 51% of women using the bureau had experienced sexual harassment in previous posts
- The Industrial Society's own survey in 1993 found that 54% of women and around 15% of men employees who responded to the survey had suffered some form of sexual harassment

> **Case law**
> Gates v. Security Guards Express. A security officer who was subjected to homosexual harassment was unlawfully discriminated against and was awarded £4,500 compensation.

DEVELOPING A POLICY ON HARASSMENT

It is essential to protect people from harassment because:

- harassment tends to get worse if it is not dealt with
- it is a major contributor to stress at work
- it causes absenteeism and job changing that reflects badly on the employment record of the person who feels they have to resort to these tactics
- without policies, those who complain run the risk of retaliation and possible loss of their job
- by doing nothing management and individuals are tacitly supporting those who harass

The management need to draw up a statement and policy in consultation with staff, develop a training programme on dealing with harassment and develop procedures for dealing with grievances and disciplinary action.

DEFINITIONS

Write definitions of what constitutes unacceptable behaviour and what may constitute harassment and discrimination (see p. 192) and adopt them as part of a code of conduct or groundrules for the organisation. Make harassment a disciplinary offence. Groundrules can be used as part of meetings procedure, training courses or for general conduct.

Definitions

Discrimination
Actions that have the effect of treating employees less favourably on the grounds of sex, marital status or race (and other grounds that can be decided on, for example sexuality).

Racial harassment
Violence (which may be verbal or physical and includes attacks on property as well as on the person) suffered by individuals or groups because of their colour, race, nationality or ethnic or national origins, when the victim believes that the perpetrator was acting on racial grounds, and/or there is evidence of racism. (Commission for Racial Equality)

Sexual harassment
May include unreciprocated and unwelcome contact, looks, physical contact or suggestions such as requests for sexual favours. It is behaviour that is objectionable and offensive to the victim and might threaten their job security and create a hostile or intimidating working environment that may very well hinder the victim in their work performance. (Equal Opportunities Commission)

Heterosexist harassment
Harassment that is directed towards lesbians or gay men, specifically or in general, in which their being lesbian or gay or beliefs held by them to be relevant to their being lesbian or gay are belittled, compared unfavourably with heterosexuality, or in any way negatively represented. Harassment may exist whether

> the act was conscious or not, and whether or not the specific employee alleging harassment is named by the harasser or is the intended recipient of the harassment. (GLC report)
>
> **Harassment of people with disabilities**
> Unwelcome terms, comments, actions or behaviour relating to a person's physical or mental abilities that are found offensive and as a result of which an unpleasant or intimidating environment is created.

PUBLICITY

Publicise these definitions and the consequences of such behaviour to workers, volunteers, senior management and clients as appropriate.

TRAINING

Train workers and volunteers in how to handle discriminatory comments or behaviour from users or clients, and train line managers to recognise harassment and to support any person who complains to them.

POLICY AND PROCEDURE

Appropriate managers should be involved in drawing up a specific procedure for dealing with harassment or discrimination (see below). Consider bringing in outsiders trained to deal with such cases.

ALLEGATIONS

Take allegations seriously. As well as being potentially unlawful, harassment can greatly affect the morale and performance of employees. Don't assume that people making allegations are being over-sensitive.

THE INVESTIGATION

The investigation of all grievances of this type must be carried out quickly and properly. The starting point should be the victim's perception of events. If they believe that a certain act was designed to harass them owing to their race, sex, sexuality or disability, then that belief must form the basis of the investigation. All other matters should be dealt with separately.

The investigation must establish:

- was the act under question harassing and causing grievance?
- was it racially or sexually motivated or motivated by prejudice against lesbians, gay men or people with disabilities?
- would someone in a similar situation but of a different race, sex, sexuality, or physical or mental ability have been treated similarly?
- has the harassment caused a deterioration in the employee's job performance?

Employees should be provided with sympathetic counselling.

REDRESS

Take action to redress the injury and discrimination suffered by the victim by preparing a plan of action with them and carrying it out. It could involve for example:

- taking disciplinary action against the perpetrator
- changing reporting or working relationships
- relocating the harasser, but with no material advantage
- maintaining a record of all incidents for future analysis

Deal promptly with racist or other offensive graffiti, regardless of whether or not a complaint is made about them.

MONITORING

Monitor and review the procedures and the nature of the complaints, and prepare an annual report of all grievances for review by senior staff or the equal opportunities committee.

EQUAL OPPORTUNITIES

Resolving Harassment Complaints

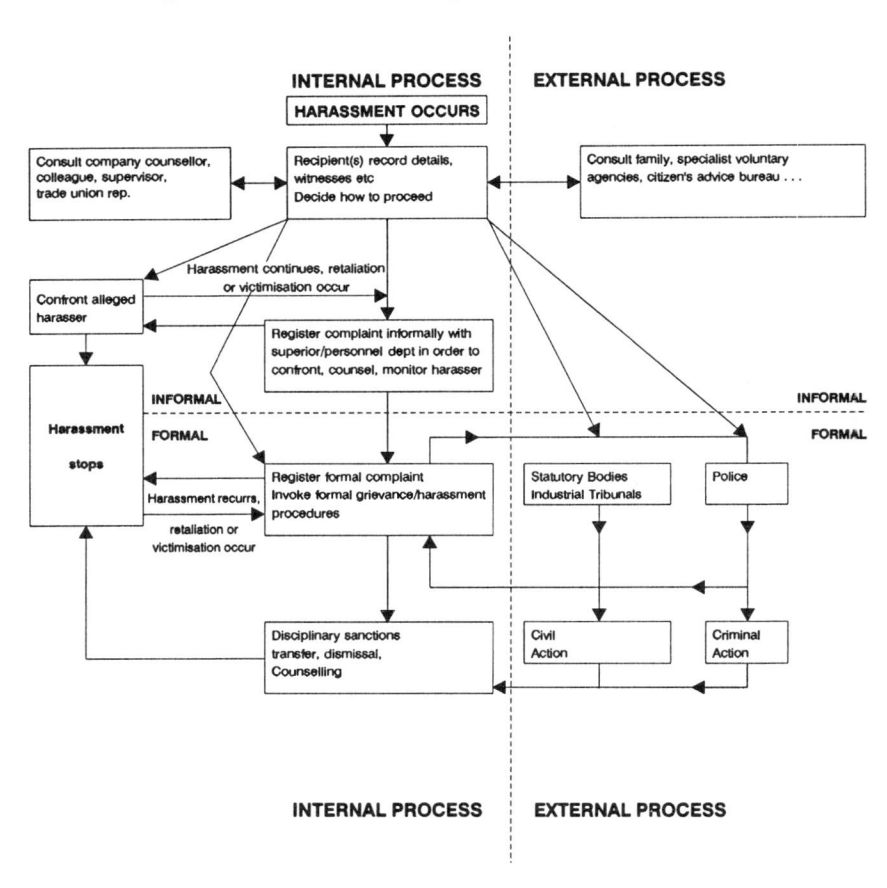

INTERNAL PROCESS	EXTERNAL PROCESS

HARASSMENT OCCURS

- Consult company counsellor, colleague, supervisor, trade union rep.
- Recipient(s) record details, witnesses etc. Decide how to proceed
- Consult family, specialist voluntary agencies, citizen's advice bureau ...

Harassment continues, retaliation or victimisation occur

- Confront alleged harasser
- Register complaint informally with superior/personnel dept in order to confront, counsel, monitor harasser

INFORMAL / FORMAL

- Harassment stops
- Register formal complaint. Invoke formal grievance/harassment procedures
- Statutory Bodies Industrial Tribunals
- Police

Harassment recurs, retaliation or victimisation occur

- Disciplinary sanctions transfer, dismissal, Counselling
- Civil Action
- Criminal Action

INTERNAL PROCESS	EXTERNAL PROCESS

Extract from *Statement on Harassment at Work*
Published by the Institute of Personnel Management

EMPLOYEE'S ACTION IN CASES OF HARASSMENT

If a person is experiencing harassment, the following suggestions recommended by the EOC in the case of sexual harassment may be helpful in providing guidelines for action.

- the harasser should be told to desist from further unacceptable conduct

- the management should be informed immediately — make use of the grievance procedure where appropriate

- the person being harassed should keep a diary of incidents so that these can be recalled accurately at an organisational enquiry or any subsequent industrial tribunal

- the person affected should confide in a colleague and inform the union or employee representative and ask for support — it may be that other people have suffered similar harassment

- advice should be sought from, e.g. the Equal Opportunities Commission, the Commission for Racial Equality, the Lesbian and Gay Employment Rights project

- indecent assault should be reported to the police

Some people may need encouragement to define their individual experiences as harassment. This is another reason why autonomous support groups are necessary at work. Anyone who is facing harassment can then gain support and discuss courses of action within the safety of the group if they feel they cannot bring it to line management directly.

PROCEDURES

Procedures for dealing with any complaint of harassment must take as their starting point that the complainant is believed. Never dismiss any complaint as unreasonable because you do not regard it as harassment — the point is that the person complaining does regard it as such.

> **Case law**
> Bracebridge Engineering v. Derby, 1990. An employee complained of sexual harassment by two supervisors. The employer failed to treat the matter seriously or investigate it properly. The Employment Appeals Tribunal found for constructive dismissal.

For the system to work, people need to have confidence that the policy and procedures have been developed in order to deal with the problem, not as a cosmetic exercise. People will be deterred from using these policies if the complainant is treated as the 'problem' employee rather than the harasser. Unfortunately this often happens, because management are unsure of the issues, not trained to deal with harassment and would rather the issue didn't exist.

For example:
Line managers failed to support staff who had frequently complained about the finance director. Complaints about his appalling attitudes, bad manners and foul language were repeatedly dismissed. Over a period of 12 months, 14 previously valued and respected staff either faced instant dismissal or handed in their notice, simply to escape his reign of terror.

- find out exactly what happened and listen to the person's complaint from beginning to end
- explain the policy on harassment and sort out the most appropriate action
- record the interview and keep it confidential
- take the action decided upon quickly

Any delay at this stage is very serious as it is unacceptable for the person to have to continue working with the harasser unless they know that their complaint is being taken seriously and action will be taken.

Because of the sensitivity of complaints of discrimination, the CRE recommends that the following steps are taken.

INFORMAL STAGE

Allow for an initial informal approach that is not recorded in the complainant's personnel file unless they wish to pursue the matter further. It is very important at this stage to allow the person to have access to a sympathetic person in identifying and resolving problems.

Tell the employee that they can be represented by their shop steward, employee representative or an employee of their choice, and let them know that they can raise the matter direct with the personnel manager or equal opportunities adviser or a named person.

Where possible, offer interpreting facilities to persons with English as a second language who wish it.

FORMAL STAGE

If the complaint cannot be resolved informally, then ensure as far as possible that the grievance is investigated by someone independent of the department to which the grievance relates, and who has been trained to understand how racial or other discrimination and harassment take place and the hurt it can cause.

Ensure that the policy requires management to respond within a fixed time limit (not more than two weeks) and that the grievance is settled as quickly as is practicable. Make it clear that discrimination and harassment are disciplinary offences the penalty for which may include dismissal.

Communicate the outcome of the grievance, including any disciplinary action taken against the offender, to the complainant with a written undertaking that they will not be victimised or suffer any other detriment.

Employees should be informed of their legal right to apply to an industrial tribunal for a decision on the matter (within three months of the original incident) in the case of racial or sexual harassment, or harassment on the grounds of political belief or religion in Northern Ireland.

COUNSELLING

Offer counselling to employees who believe that they have suffered unfair treatment, harassment or victimisation.

GRIEVANCE AND DISCIPLINARY PANEL

The procedures that are developed must include placing people on the grievance and disciplinary panel who have experience of dealing with racial, sexual or heterosexual harassment cases. If necessary, bring in an outside person to attend the panel. The panel should be trained to deal sensitively with the issues and to have worked out any attitudes they may have towards harassment before becoming panel members.

There should, as a matter of course, be at least one woman, one black or ethnic minority person, or one lesbian or gay person on the panel, according to who has complained of harassment. Representatives may have to challenge any prejudices arising during the process of dealing with the case as well as the incident itself. The complainant must have a supporter with them at any stage of the grievance procedure to help in putting their case if necessary.

DISCIPLINARY ACTION

Once the grievance has been settled, and if the case has legitimacy, then the disciplinary procedure should be invoked against the harasser. This might result in the procedure for gross misconduct being used, which might result in suspension or dismissal. Action must also be taken to redress the injury to the complainant. If anyone is to be moved to another job within the organisation then it should be the harasser who moves and they should never gain in grade or financially out of any move.

5.4 DISCIPLINARY, GRIEVANCE AND DISMISSAL PROCEDURES

Nobody likes the idea that disciplinary and grievance procedures may be necessary in their organisation. Senior managers and management committee or board members may like even less the idea that they may have to discipline a fellow worker or hear a grievance. However, until perfect communication and standards of behaviour and conduct are achieved, disciplinary and grievance procedures will always be necessary.

Even if you think you will never need them, you should have them prepared because:

- it is a lawful requirement to have a written disciplinary and grievance procedure if more than 20 people are employed — the purpose is not to punish them but to ensure that everyone knows what the required standards are and to encourage improvement

- whether or not you followed the ACAS Code of Practice on Discipline may be taken into account by industrial tribunals

For further reading on this subject area, consult *Discipline, Grievance and Dismissal* by Sue Morris (published by the Industrial Society)

GENERAL GUIDELINES

- make every attempt to create conditions whereby problems can be sorted out informally before getting to the state of formal proceedings. This may best be achieved by including an informal process, which must be followed before formal proceedings can be invoked, in which problems are discussed by the relevant staff and any third party.

    Only in the case of gross misconduct is it appropriate for the formal procedures to be used immediately.

- develop procedures that allow for full and unbiased investigation of any allegation of misconduct or circumstances surrounding a grievance.

Such an investigation will often have to be carried out by a disciplinary and grievance panel, the membership of which is drawn from the organisation's senior managers, personnel manager or management committee or board. These members should be elected at the start of each new term of office as a standing group; they should be trained in dealing with grievances and investigations and be fully aware themselves of the procedures in force.

Disciplinary actions concerning unsatisfactory work or conduct may be initiated by the manager, but the manager should keep the panel informed of progress, and involve them once the formal written stage is reached.

- allow employees to have their employee representative, or other representative of their choice, present at any hearing in which they are involved.

- build an appeal process into the procedure after every decision has been reached to enable employees to appeal against unfavourable decisions concerning their case. It makes sense for there to be an external appeal against dismissal, as once the issue has gone that far no one in the organisation is going to be unaware of the issues, so an internal appeal process may no longer be unbiased. However, this is difficult in practice and may not be possible.

Membership of any appeals group that might be set up should be different from that of the original disciplinary and grievance panel in order to ensure an unbiased assessment.

- apprise employees of their lawful rights in the matter and their rights to apply to an industrial tribunal in the event of alleged unfair dismissal or discriminatory treatment. The relevant time limits should be made known.

- make clear to volunteers whether or not the disciplinary procedures apply to them. They should ideally be included under both disciplinary and grievance procedures, although there is no statutory obligation to do so.

GRIEVANCE PROCEDURES

Workers may need to air grievances about inconsistent pay and conditions, application of the organisation's rules, the style of management or issues relating to colleagues and their behaviour. These should be raised informally at first with the manager. But if the problem involves the manager or cannot be resolved at that level, then the issue should move swiftly to the disciplinary and grievance panel.

Grievances can cover complaints of discrimination and harassment according to definitions adopted by the organisation. All grievances under this heading should be properly investigated and dealt with as a matter of urgency (see section 3 for the best policy).

Where a matter relating to terms and conditions of employment is raised by more than one member of staff, the issue should become a matter for collective bargaining between the union and senior managers or management committee or board, and not treated as a grievance under the procedures set out here.

DISCIPLINARY PROCEDURES

The ACAS guidelines are that disciplinary procedures should:

- be in writing
- specify to whom they apply
- provide for the matter to be dealt with quickly
- indicate the disciplinary action that may be taken
- specify the levels of management that have the authority to take the various forms of disciplinary action, ensuring that immediate superiors do not normally have the power to dismiss without reference to the management committee
- provide for the individuals to be informed of the complaints against them and to be given an opportunity to state their case before decisions are reached
- give individuals the right to be accompanied by a trade union representative or a fellow employee of their choice
- ensure that, except in cases of gross misconduct, no employee is dismissed for a first breach of discipline
- ensure that disciplinary action is not taken until the case has been carefully investigated
- ensure that individuals are given an explanation for any penalty imposed
- provide a right of appeal and specify the procedure to be followed

When a disciplinary situation arises, the first task is to make sure of the facts of the case, as quickly as possible, before memories fade. If the case is serious, then the employee can be suspended while the investigation is carried out. Before any action is taken or sanctions imposed, the employee must be interviewed and allowed to state their case and be informed of their rights under the disciplinary procedure.

The normal sequence of warnings recommended by the ACAS code is as follows:

1. formal oral warning for minor offences — the employee should be warned that this constitutes the first step of a disciplinary procedure and the likely consequence of further offences
2. formal written warning if the offence is more serious
3. final written warning for further misconduct — state that any reoccurrence will lead to suspension or dismissal.

DISMISSAL

It is unlawful and contrary to equal opportunities principles to discriminate in the application of disciplinary procedures or to make use of them to victimise a person who brings a grievance against the organisation under the Sex Discrimination Act, the Race Relations Act or the Equal Pay Act, or to victimise someone who is involved in trade union activities.

PREGNANCY DISMISSAL

It is automatically unfair to dismiss a woman with two years' continuous service (five years if part time) if the principal reason for her dismissal is her pregnancy. Recent decisions of the European Court of Justice have also made it certain that any dismissal on pregnancy grounds (regardless of length of service) is a breach of the Equal Treatment Directive (Dekker v. VJV Centrum and Hertz 1990).

FAIR DISMISSAL

Five cases listed in the Employment Protection (Consolidation) Act constitute fair dismissal:

1. A reason related to the capability (including health reasons) or qualifications of the employee for performing work of the kind they were employed to do

2. A reason related to the employee's conduct

3. The employee was redundant

4. That the employee could not continue to work in the position that they held without contravention of a duty or restriction imposed by an enactment

5. Some other substantial reason of a kind to justify the dismissal of an employee holding that post — for example, the ending of a fixed-term contract, reorganisation of an organisation

To show that a dismissal is fair the employer must be able to show that there was both a fair reason for dismissal *and* that the procedure adopted was fair (see the ACAS guidelines above). In an industrial tribunal you must be able to show that you adopted and went through the procedures properly.

Criminal offences outside employment should not automatically be treated as reasons for dismissal, regardless of whether the case has any bearing on the duties of the individual as an employee. The main considerations should be whether the offence is one that makes the employee unsuitable for their type of work or unacceptable to other employees. Employees should not be dismissed solely because a charge against them is pending.

SUMMARY DISMISSAL

In certain circumstances an employee can be summarily dismissed. This should happen only after investigation and hearing the employee's side of the story. There must have been an act of gross misconduct, a major breach of duty or conduct that brings the organisation into disrepute. Examples of this are:

- a serious breach of safety rules threatening life and limb
- theft
- fraud
- being under the influence of drink or illegal drugs during working hours
- failure to follow the organisation's documented rules
- a breach of duty regarding the disclosure of confidential information
- deliberate damage to workers' or organisation's property
- acts of harassment or discrimination

Examples of your organisation should be specified in the procedures and guidelines for gross misconduct.

APPEAL PROCEDURES

It is legally necessary to have an appeal procedure after every stage of a procedure in case a grievance or disciplinary matter should not be resolved to the satisfaction of all parties. An employee who wants to appeal against dismissal should have their case reviewed by an internal committee of individuals who did not participate in the original decision to dismiss. If this fails, the individual may in the last resort contact ACAS (see the Address section in Chapter 8).

ACTION SUMMARY

- aim to avoid disciplinary and grievance proceedings by setting clear policies, procedures and management guidelines
- ensure you follow the ACAS, CRE and EOC guidelines and codes of practice on discipline and grievance
- be very careful of your legal position regarding dismissal

But remember, Don't

- use dismissal in an unfair or discriminatory way
- ignore cases that come to your attention

5.6 ACTION SUMMARY

- ensure you are offering anti-discriminatory terms and conditions

- adopt a company wide continuous development, staff development or career development programme for all employees, set targets and monitor it to make sure discrimination is still not operating

- publish policies on promotion, regrading, training and transfers and make them clear to all staff and line managers

- write definitions of what constitutes unacceptable behaviour, harassment and discrimination and adopt them as part of a code of conduct or ground rules for the organisation. Make harassment a disciplinary offence

- aim to avoid disciplinary and grievance by setting clear policies, procedures and management guidelines

- ensure you follow the ACA, CRE and EOC guidelines and codes of practice on disciplinary and grievance

CONTRACTUAL RIGHTS

Do

- make sure that your terms and conditions are fair to all workers, especially part timers

- consider developing contractual options on for example

paternity and co-parent leave

parental responsibility leave

carers' leave

childcare and carers' costs

childcare and caring subsidy

But remember, Don't

- deliberately offer worse rights to part-timers or women

STAFF DEVELOPMENT

Do

- ensure your appraisal system is open and participative

- assess problem areas in the company where different groups are underrepresented at senior levels or in access to career development

- develop a corporate strategy involving: support, supervision, appraisal, identifying learning and training needs, in-house training, external training, learning on the job, mentoring, coaching continuous development

- develop a clear policy and priorities on access to resources for training and consider the need for positive action training

- develop accelerated development and training schemes for women and black staff if they are underrepresented

- encourage line managers to encourage underrepresented groups to take advantage of company opportunities for training and development, throughout the staff development policy.

But remember, Don't

- make stereotyped assumptions about people's motivations at different staff grades, across one sex or race of employee. Ask about their circumstances and make sure you don't rule people out for promotion or training for spurious reasons.

HARASSMENT

Do

- publicise definitions of harassment and the consequences of such behaviour to workers, volunteers, management committee or board members, users or clients as appropriate.
- train people in how to handle discriminatory comments or behaviour from users or clients.
- take all allegations seriously.
- investigate all grievances of this type quickly and properly.
- provide employees with sympathetic counselling.

But remember, Don't

- ignore incidents or pretend they aren't happening
- tell individuals that 'It's just a joke', 'It's just his manner', You've got a chip on your shoulder!'
- dismiss or victimise people because they complain of harassment.

DISCIPLINARY AND GRIEVANCE PROCEDURES

Do

- always follow organisation procedures
- be very careful of your legal position regarding dismissal

But remember, Don't

- use dismissal in an unfair or discriminatory way
- ignore cases that come to your attention.

5.7 LEGAL SUMMARY

EMPLOYMENT, PROMOTION, TRANSFERS AND REGRADING

The **Sex Discrimination Act 1975**, the **Race Relations Act 1976** and the **Fair Employment (NI) Act** make it unlawful to discriminate in the terms of employment, benefits, facilities and service offered to employees.

The **EOC Code of Practice** suggests some options for positive action in employment such as: offering part-time or flexi-time working; personal leave arrangements open to both sexes so that men can undertake domestic responsibilities; enhanced statutory maternity leave provisions.

The **CRE Code of Practice** recommends that extended leave provisions for employees should be developed and applied consistently to ensure that they are not discriminatory.

The **Equal Pay Act 1970** entitles employees not to suffer inequality in contractual terms on the grounds of sex, by incorporating an equality clause into contracts.

The **Trade Union Reform and Employment Rights Act 1993** confers new maternity rights from October 1994.

HARASSMENT

Harassment has been held to constitute discrimination under the **Race Relations Act,** the **Sex Discrimination Act** and the **Fair Employment (NI) Act**.

The EC has issued a declaration on the intention to implement a Council recommendation on the dignity of men and women at work, including a Code of Practice to combat sexual harassment.

The European Court of Justice ruled in August 1993 that there is now no fixed upper limit (previously it had been £11,000) on the compensation recoverable by a victim of sex discrimination in respect of loss and damage sustained.

Employers are *prima facie* liable for what their employees do in the course of their employment, whether or not the employer knows of those actions. Employers can avoid claims for liability only if they can prove that they took measures to ensure that the offending acts were not done. *Race Relations Act, Sex Discrimination Act, Fair Employment (NI) Act as above.*

Harassment may also lead to criminal claims for assault or civil claims for negligence or breach of contract. For example, harassment may lead to employees resigning and bringing claims for constructive dismissal. *Employment Protection (Consolidation) Act 1978*

Specific statutory provisions allow employees to claim if they were harassed because of their trade union membership or activities or non-membership. *Trade Union and Labour Relations (Consolidation) Act 1992.*

DISCIPLINARY AND GRIEVANCE PROCEDURES

Unfair dismissal is covered under the **Employment Protection Consolidation Act 1978** and the ACAS guidelines on disciplinary and grievance procedures.

PREGNANCY DISMISSAL

It is automatically unfair to dismiss a woman with two years' continuous service (five years if part time) if the principal reason for her dismissal is her pregnancy. Recent decisions of the European Court of Justice have also made it certain that any dismissal on pregnancy grounds (regardless of length of service) is a breach of the Equal Treatment Directive (**Dekker v. VJV Centrum and Hertz 1990**).

6 FLEXIBLE WORKING

Flexible working patterns are on the increase not only in the UK but also across Europe. The impulse for this may be the recession and the cost-saving elements of flexible working arrangements. However, the benefits of increasing the options for workers and employers are leading to greater use of this form of working. This chapter considers management issues and the benefits and costs of introducing flexible working, and looks at some of the most common forms.

KEY CONCEPTS

- job sharing
- teleworking
- term-time working

QUESTIONS ANSWERED

- am I legally obliged to offer a job-share?
- what is the difference between job sharing and part-time working?
- what is the best way to organise core time and flexi-time?
- how can I ensure that I don't lose management control over the work?
- who should be able to apply for the schemes?

CONTENTS

1: **Management of flexible working**
    Why offer flexible terms?
    Benefits to workers or potential workers
    Benefits to the organisation
        Costs
    Strategy and planning
        Impact
    Access
        Practical issues
2: **Forms of flexible working**
    Job sharing and job splitting
        Definitions
        Main Points
        Benefits to the organisation
        Management issues
        Legal issues and employment protection rights for job sharers
        Sample guidelines
    Part-time employment
        Definition
        Main points
        Benefits to the organisation
        Management issues
        Employment terms for part-time staff
    Working from home or teleworking
        Definitions
        Main points
        Benefits to the organisation
        Management issues
        Legal issues
3: **Action summary**
4: **Legal summary**

6.1 MANAGEMENT OF FLEXIBLE WORKING

WHY OFFER FLEXIBLE TERMS?

The pattern of working 9 to 5, five days a week is a formula deeply ingrained in society. It is assumed that variations from this are somehow not as productive or as valuable, and that not as much value should be given to the people who want or need to work different hours. Such assumptions stem from deeply entrenched attitudes and hinder any desire to facilitate workers' productivity, especially women's, in a changing society.

This approach to the working week is predicated on the sexist way society has been organised. Men traditionally go out to work and women work at home for no wages, keeping the social structure intact and enabling the economy to survive. Society is changing, however, and men and women are demanding a different economic relationship to home and work. Employers can help or hinder these changes. If they are inflexible, then they are likely to lose good workers to firms that do offer flexible working deals.

Attitudes to part-time work have also been a hindrance. Doing a job part-time does not mean people are doing it half as competently or that it is half as important as a full-time job, although this is often reflected in the fact that part-time workers are paid less on average by the hour than full-time staff performing the same work.

BENEFITS TO WORKERS OR POTENTIAL WORKERS

Almost every worker at some point in their lives would benefit from some form of flexible working arrangement. Domestic and other responsibilities vary from time to time, which means that people may prefer different working arrangements at different times in their working lives.

The following groups would benefit particularly:

- people with caring responsibilities
- people with disabilities
- people with particular cultural or religious needs (people who have to observe special times for prayer, holy days, special holidays and dietary requirements)

Employers can both retain staff and attract new staff by adopting a flexible attitude towards working arrangements.

For example:
Paula suffered a back injury that means that she is now in constant pain. She can control this, but needs to work reduced hours with an opportunity to have frequent breaks. She is now working part time, spreading her working hours out over five days to facilitate her need for rest periods.

BENEFITS TO THE ORGANISATION

- you retain experienced staff
- you can cut recruitment costs
- you might want to have the option for yourself one day
- possibility of greater skills mix
- happier workers
- more flexible workforce to meet business needs

- greater freedom to organise the working week round how people live their lives
- travelling might be easier at off peak times
- travel costs could be less

COSTS

- job sharers cost more than one person
- managers are managing more complex arrangements and maybe more people
- you may lose experienced workers if they can't work flexi-time with you but have to for personal reasons, and therefore leave to go to another employer

STRATEGY AND PLANNING

If you're going to introduce flexible working then the whole organisation must adopt a policy that applies to all staff. This avoids accusations of 'favouritism or special treatment' levelled at line managers. The personnel department or wages department will need to be involved in the recording of flexi-hours and calculations of take-home pay.

IMPACT

Once the policy is in place, managers have to consider the overall impact of requests to work flexibly. Setting core times and flexible times must be done for the convenience of the organisation not of individual employees. Adopting a flexible working policy is not a way of solving individuals' family or domestic problems. It may benefit certain individuals but that is not a sufficient reason to adopt the scheme in the first place.

A heavier burden might be placed on managers because they have to decide when staff can take flexi-days, arrange cover more flexibly, and manage more interactions over different times of working. Managers will not themselves be able to work throughout the whole of the flexi-day and so some employees might work without supervision. Inadequate supervision might lead to abuse of the system, which is an important factor to consider when thinking of introducing any scheme.

It is important in implementing any change that negative attitudes towards variable working hours are not reinforced by some people in the organisation. For example, people answering phone enquiries should be trained not to say, 'They are not here, they only work part-time', but to say when they will be there and to ask if anyone else could help.

ACCESS

Who can apply to take advantage of these arrangements? Do they apply to all staff in all types of posts in all grades or only some?

For example, posts with line management responsibilities for other staff need to be 'on hand' at the office more than some other posts.

If they don't apply to all staff, then what are the criteria for deciding who can apply for them and in what circumstances? Such criteria must be carefully worked out to avoid suggestions of unfair treatment. It could be possible to offer the options as a possibility if the conditions are suitable, not as a right.

PRACTICAL ISSUES

Managers will have to ensure cover and consistent opening hours as a priority and plan ahead so that covering office hours on Fridays in the summer does not become a problem if all workers decide they want the same long weekend.

Term-time working It may be difficult to provide cover for the school holidays and could place a burden on full-time/full-year workers.

Management of job sharers The line management structure needs to be carefully worked out for each job-share post. This should include individual staff support and supervision for each postholder and some joint meetings with both postholders and line manager.

The line manager needs to have an outline of the hours planned to be worked every month in advance and to be informed of any changes.

Both postholders should be encouraged to attend all team meetings and other meetings involving all staff, particularly in the first several months, acknowledging that this may not always be possible owing to hours/days worked. There may be times when one postholder is expected to cover for the other in this type of meeting.

6.2 FORMS OF FLEXIBLE WORKING

The phase 'flexible working' covers a variety of ways of working that can be adapted to suit individual needs for choice over the number and arrangements of hours worked. The forms of flexible working covered here are:

job sharing and job splitting,
working from home or teleworking

JOB SHARING AND JOB SPLITTING

DEFINITIONS

Job sharing is generally defined as an arrangement where one full-time job is shared by two people, with the responsibilities and benefits of the job being shared equally between them.

Some jobs are split on a week on, week off arrangement, some on the basis of two and a half days each. It is important to have some overlap time when people are sharing jobs, and many organisations offer three days work to each worker rather than two and a half days to allow for this.

Job splitting is where a job is divided into two jobs, each with defined areas of responsibility and done by different part-time workers. This is often easier to manage and control.

MAIN POINTS

- job sharing involves two people doing one job, bringing two sets of skills, abilities and styles to the job

- it allows for different forms of working to be agreed by the partners; for example, mornings and afternoons, 2.5 days per week each, or alternate weeks

- it could be possible with the agreement of the partners to ask them to work at the same time to cover busy periods of the week, and then split the rest of the time between them. It would be possible to employ a person with disabilities to do the half of the job that they find most suitable and someone else to do the other half.

For example:
Jack wants to spend time at home with his children before they go to school; Gill wants to have time to study and work for her MBA. They both independently decide to apply to job share the post of finance officer.

This job is eminently suitable for sharing and it is agreed that they can both apply for the next internal vacancy that comes up.

BENEFITS TO THE ORGANISATION

- a greater range of skills is made available
- it allows for more flexibility of skills and working time
- it permits the retention of experienced staff, e.g. maternity returners, carers, people with disabilities, people who wish to study or work less than full time for any other reason
- it can be introduced for any grade of job
- it can apply to different sorts of contract — permanent, fixed-term, consultants, etc

MANAGEMENT ISSUES

It is important to set clear groundrules for who can apply and in what circumstances (for example, internal applicants, external requests, do they have to apply with a partner or not?)

A clear division of roles and responsibilities is needed, which may require closer line management. In addition, line managers have to manage two people instead of one.

It is necessary to sort out clear terms and conditions of work, for example on: hours of work and continuous employment rights, rates of pay, overtime or time off in lieu, holidays (including bank holidays), sick pay, maternity leave, paternity leave, cover for sharer, change-over and overlap time, job sharer leaving, redundancy, return to full-time work.

LEGAL ISSUES AND EMPLOYMENT PROTECTION RIGHTS FOR JOB SHARERS

Each worker needs a separate contract, and you need to be careful not to fall foul of conditions for retaining statutory employment rights.

There is no automatic right to be able to job share. However it may be deemed indirect sex discrimination not to be able to apply to return to part-time work or job sharing upon returning from maternity leave. This applies only to women and not to men wishing to job share.

> **Case law**
> Clay v. The Governors English Martyrs School 1993. The Leicester industrial tribunal upheld a complaint that the refusal to allow a teacher to jobshare on her return from maternity leave was indirect sex discrimination. The tribunal also rejected the argument that job sharing among teachers is not in the educational interests of children.

Certain statutory employment rights, such as the right not to be unfairly dismissed or maternity rights (see Chapter 7), depend upon certain continuous lengths of service having been completed with one employer. Under Schedule 13 of the **Employment Protection (Consolidation) Act 1978**, weeks will count only if the employee:

- works for 16 or more hours a week or is employed under a contract that normally involves 16 or more hours a week

- works under a contract that normally involves 8 or more hours a week but less than 16 and has done so continuously for five years

- used to work under a contract that normally involved 16 or more hours a week, but now works under a contract normally involving between 8 and 16 hours a week (subject to a maximum of 26 weeks short-time working between each period of normal working)

Certain working arrangements may run into difficulties:

- employees working two days one week and three the next. If the normal working day is less than 8 hours, the two-day week will fall below the 16-hour threshold and continuity will be broken unless the employee has worked for more than five years.

- alternate-week working which falls foul of the same provision.

Sample guidelines

1. Introduction

The company has instituted a policy of job sharing as part of its implementation of equal opportunities, and as a recognition that job sharing is an efficient and desirable way of using human resources

2. How job shares can be set up

Posts can be shared in a variety of ways:

A Two candidates can apply for a vacant post and both be successful.

B One successful candidate can be appointed to a post on a job-share basis, and the remaining portion re-advertised.

C Two separate candidates can be appointed to a vacant post on a job-share basis.

D An existing postholder can request their post be job shared and the remaining portion be advertised as a job-share post.

E An employee returning from maternity leave or long-term sick leave or a newly disabled existing postholder who wishes to undertake part-time work can do so in their post as a job sharer, and the remaining portion would then be advertised.

3. Hours and work arrangements

The best guide to these is feasibility and this will differ from post to post.

Hours

No formulae are laid down and hours can be organised to suit both the service and the employee. However, managers should consider that wherever an arrangement of work hours is being settled, the hours/days/weeks agreed with either job sharer should always be such that, should a part vacancy occur, the working hours arrangement will form a sufficiently viable package to attract new would-be job sharers at the earliest possible time.

It should also be borne in mind by all parties that employment protection is currently lost where the hours fall below 16 a week. This will change in due course following a recent House of Lords decision. See Legal Summary on page 242.

4. Duties and responsibilities

There are no rules or preferred options on this. The aim in all cases is to adopt the best mode for ensuring efficiency. Therefore division may be into projects, tasks, clients or merely time.

All parties should take great care not to confuse working arrangements with the job description. The latter is what is being shared and, although the duties are being divided, the overall responsibility will always be shared. Without this understanding it might be possible for one partner to monopolise the most prestigious areas of work.

5. Adjustments to working arrangements

These should be handled with the same care and sensitivity using the same principles as for full-time workers, who would not expect their working patterns to be altered without full consultation.

Where one partner may be absent from work for any reason, there is no contractual right of management to expect the other partner to cover.

Where the partner has been informally approached and agrees to cover for the absent colleague, if time over and above contractual hours is involved, the extra time will count as time off in lieu. These arrangements must be agreed in advance with the line manager.

Line managers must be aware that when changes to study or childcare arrangements (for example) are necessary, additional expenses may be incurred, and it may not be reasonable to expect job-share partners to make changes to arrangements at short notice.

Where overlap periods have been agreed in order to facilitate communication between job sharers, and the requirement of the service is for cover throughout every working day, time off in lieu should be granted for extra hours worked or the total number of hours worked should slightly exceed the regular full-time hours.

6. Accommodation

Where the sharers have divided the hours and working arrangements in such a way that they do not work at the same time, or where overlap periods are less than half a day, one standard desk is all that is necessary plus one extra chair. But where 35 hours are concentrated into a lesser number of days and the partners are working simultaneously for a more substantial part of the time, they are entitled to a desk and chair each, and cupboard and filing space appropriate to the needs of the post.

Where the time spent within the office area is not substantial, other ad hoc arrangements may be made by agreement.

Lack of accommodation is not a reason to refuse a job share.

7. Notice periods

Job sharing is open to all employees and existing employees may request to share their own posts. Two months' notice in writing must be given and the line manager must reply within two weeks.

Sympathetic consideration may be given to emergencies, and of course it is open to management or the employee to reduce or extend the notice period by mutual agreement. For example, it might be helpful to managers if the job sharer were to remain in post full time until a partner was in post, but this must never become a condition, and the post should be advertised without delay.

8. Selection and interviewing

Training

It will be necessary to train selection panel members on the specific requirements of interviewing and selecting where job-share applicants are involved.

Consultation

When part of a job-share post becomes vacant there is not the same opportunity for the job description to be reviewed as is the case with a full-time vacancy, because job sharers have the same job description and the post is not actually vacant.

The remaining job sharer should be involved in any review of the working arrangements and be consulted about the advertising stages, but not about the person specification or the selection or interviewing stage. The degree of consultation will obviously increase in ratio to the complexity and sensitivity of the duties and responsibilities of the post.

Interview procedure
For applicants who wish to be considered as job sharers:

(A) Individual applicants:
They should be treated exactly the same as all other candidates up to the final decision, when they should be assessed with every other candidate who has applied to job share as well as on their own.

(B) Joint job-share applicants:
They should be treated exactly the same as other candidates up to the interview, when an additional joint interview will be held. At the final decision they should be assessed firstly with the job-share partner they have applied with and secondly with each other person who has applied to job share.

Where candidates are being given a 30-minute interview, a joint job-share application is treated as follows:

20 minutes for each applicant individually
20 minutes together to assess the feasibility of a job share

Interviewers are entitled at the end of the interviews to make any selection according to assessed ability. For example:

to appoint one applicant full time
to appoint a joint job-share application
to appoint one half of a joint job-share application either with another job-share application, or on their own and then to advertise the other half as necessary
to appoint a single applicant for job share and then to advertise the other half

Application form
There should be a separate section on the application form for job applicants to make it known that they are interested in job sharing.

Advertising
All job adverts to which the policy applies will contain the phrase: 'job-sharing applications welcome'.

An A4 sheet containing a summary of the company's policy on job sharing will be sent out as background information to all applicants as part of the jobs package.

9. <u>Management</u>

The line management structure needs to be carefully worked out for each job-share post. This will include individual staff support and supervision for each postholder and some joint meetings with both postholders and line manager.

The line manager needs to have an outline of the hours planned to be worked every month in advance and to be informed of any changes.

Both postholders will be encouraged to attend all team meetings, and other meetings involving all staff, particularly in the first several months, acknowledging that this may not always be possible owing to hours/days worked. There may be times when the postholders are expected to cover for each other in this type of meeting.

10. Terms and conditions

All terms and conditions apply pro rata as outlined in the contract of employment, including salary, sick pay, entitlement to holidays, bridging days and bank holidays, and other conditions of employment.

Both postholders are subject to a probationary period of three months extendable to six months. A review of the working of the job-share arrangements will take place after six months.

11. Training

Access to training courses must be allocated on an individual and not a pro rata basis.

Line managers should also consider if it would be beneficial to train the job sharers simultaneously, using the time off in lieu provisions.

12. What happens when a job sharer leaves

A policy must be adopted by the company. One option is to offer the job share to the other postholder on a full-time basis. They will have one month after the receipt of the offer to accept in writing. If they do not wish to do this, the remaining hours of the post will be advertised.

PART-TIME WORKING

DEFINITION

There is no agreed definition, except that workers work less than normal full-time hours.

MAIN POINTS

There are various options of part-time working that you could make available to your staff. These could include the following forms:

- **Permanent reduction in hours**
  You could offer the right to any member of staff to request a permanent reduction in working hours to a minimum of 16 hours per week.

  The format for the request and time deadlines within which to expect a reply would have to be worked out.

  The line manager would look at how the responsibilities of the post could be covered. This could be by instituting a job-share arrangement, by offering extra hours to other postholders or by de-prioritising some of the work areas. The request should then be discussed at the senior management team meetings to look at team implications.

  If the request is approved by the line manager and senior managers, then the arrangement must be brought in by a certain specified time after the date of that meeting.

  All terms and conditions of employment for permanent staff should apply, pro rata where relevant. Any permanent change in hours worked

should not affect the worker's entitlement to continuous employment rights.

- **Temporary reduction in hours**
  You might allow members of staff to request a temporary reduction in hours for a maximum of six months to cover personal changes in circumstances. The same criteria and time limits apply as above.

- **Term-time working**
  Arrangements can often be difficult during the school holidays for those with young children. Organisations could consider making a leave provision for parents to take extra time off during school holidays, to work at home, or to vary their hours at these times.

  If employees are given unpaid leave of absence during the school holidays, they have the same terms and conditions as permanently contracted full- and part-time staff. Staff work 40 or 41 weeks in any year.

  In order to apply, staff would follow the requirements for a permanent reduction in hours.

- **Flexible working hours including core times**
  In this case, staff work the specified number of hours per week in their contract, but can spread them over the week as they choose, subject to office opening times, core times and cover arrangements.

  By instituting flexible with 'core hours', organisations can be sure of having all staff present at certain times and allowing individual workers to vary their work times to suit themselves. A 'core hours' system is one where all workers are expected to be at work between certain hours, for example between 11 am and 3 pm, except when they are taking leave. Some people may prefer to work slightly more hours one day and slightly fewer the next.

Some organisations adopt flexitime for some staff but exclude others, usually the lower-scale staff (especially receptionists or telephonists). With thought and care all staff can be included in such a system and arrangements for cover can be organised.

> **A sample contract clause**
>
> You are required to work 35 hours per week (excluding lunch times), but these may be spread over the week in a flexible way.
>
> The office is open for work from 8.30 am to 18.30 pm, Monday to Friday.
>
> Core time is 10.00 am to 15.00 pm.
>
> Staff must take a lunch break of at least half an hour, and may take up to two hours between 12.00 and 14.00 pm.
>
> Staff are required to arrange their hours of work in discussion with their line manager and other staff in their team as appropriate on a fortnightly planning basis, and to be subject to the demands of providing cover for different areas of work first and foremost.
>
> In a four-week period, staff may accrue credit or debit hours up to a maximum of five hours, which may be carried forward no further than the next four-week accounting period.

- **Nine-day fortnight**
  The nine-day fortnight allows individuals to work their contractual hours over nine working days instead of the usual ten. The tenth day off is agreed in advance with the line manager and is granted in accordance with the cover and workload commitments of the team.

  This way of working only really works if core and flexitime arrangements are in place already.

  Any staff wishing to work under this arrangement should apply to their immediate line manager and discuss how they would fit the hours into the core, flexitime and cover arrangements.

  BENEFITS TO THE ORGANISATION

  - flexibility
  - you retain staff who might not be willing or able to work full time
  - it may be possible to manage the hours of part-time workers to meet periods of greater need

  MANAGEMENT ISSUES

  - the hassles of managing staff working flexible hours require good planning
  - the information needs of staff are greater and need to be efficiently managed
  - you need to decide who can apply for which scheme and whether some workers are more likely to benefit from it than others

EMPLOYMENT TERMS FOR PART-TIME STAFF

Hourly rates of pay should be the same as for full-time workers. People who are taken on for part-time work should ideally be taken on for at least 16 hours per week so that they qualify for full employment rights. Specific terms and conditions should be extended to them so that they do not face discrimination in access to benefits enjoyed by full-time workers. In general, as many terms and conditions as possible should be extended to cover part-time workers in full and not pro rata. Some specific examples of good practice follow.

- **Annual leave**
  Staff who work part time should have leave paid on a pro rata basis. However, where a person works reduced hours over five days a week, then they should be entitled to the same number of days' annual leave as full-timers, as the organisation loses nothing by granting this.

- **Sick pay and sick leave**
  Part-time staff should receive full sick leave entitlement, but sick pay should be reduced pro rata. Owing to Statutory Sick Pay (SSP) rules, some part-time staff may not be eligible for SSP either because they are not sick for long enough to qualify or because they do not earn enough to meet the minimum earnings requirement for SSP. It is important therefore that organisations should include all staff, especially part-time staff, in any sick pay scheme or health insurance scheme that they are part of. Guarantee of income during periods of sickness is as crucial to part-timers as it is to full-timers.

- **Pensions and life assurance schemes**
  A recent study by the EOC showed that women are discriminated against in the type and level of benefits in employers' pensions and life assurance schemes. It is important to equalise benefits for full-time and part-time staff. Organisations should look at their schemes to ensure that they are relevant and equal. This is particularly important for part-time workers, who are unlikely to take out this sort of cover themselves.

WORKING FROM HOME OR TELEWORKING

DEFINITIONS

Workers work from their own home for some or all of the week or for the duration of a particular task. Teleworking is a term used when staff use new technology to enable them to work from home or work away from the office. This form of working may well increase for some types of workers in the future.

Where possible, it can help people with caring responsibilities to be able to work at home for some periods of time.

MAIN POINTS

Only some jobs will be suitable for working from home or teleworking — jobs that are self-contained and require little face-to-face contact and little interaction with colleagues (for example, computer staff, salespeople who need to travel a lot).

Perhaps only some parts of some jobs from time to time may be eligible — for example, writing lengthy reports, newsletters or books, carrying out phone surveys initiated by the company, analysing survey or monitoring/evaluation results, performing annual budgeting or cashflow work, other tasks as appropriate.

Maybe some workers would rather not work from home! Not all homes or home circumstances are suitable.

BENEFITS TO THE ORGANISATION

- savings on travel costs
- savings on desk space
- less stressed staff
- some staff with caring responsibilities might be enabled to work more easily

MANAGEMENT ISSUES

As workers are based at a distance from the central office, they may be more divorced from the staff team generally and can't be supervised on a day-to-day basis. As a result, you may lose team feeling and cohesion, and other workers may be jealous or resentful of the one given the 'privilege of working from home'.

It is therefore important to set performance standards and to check they are being stuck to. You will have to trust people to do the work under their own steam and without a lot of support.

There will also be increased expenditure on overheads at the worker's home, fewer bodies in the office to share the routine chores, and less face-to-face time available for clients.

Who can apply to work from home, and how, will have to be decided and the terms and conditions of how many hours worked over what number of days will need to be worked out.

LEGAL ISSUES

Workers would be employed under contract and not self-employed. Managers should ensure that any office equipment under loan was covered in the insurance cover.

6.3 ACTION SUMMARY

- organise a planning and strategy meeting to discuss a flexible working policy if it's not already in place
- publicise what is available to all workers
- make clear who can apply for which form of flexible working entitlement
- set clear terms and conditions of service in the office letter or change of post letter
- try and ensure that part-timers don't lose out on statutory or company sickness, maternity or pension schemes
- make sure the conditions are advertised in the recruitment process

Do

- plan the entitlements that you can sensibly offer
- make the policy available for all workers to see what they can apply for
- ensure that the work that is being done can be checked for quality
- ensure that other workers don't undermine the part-timer or one working from home by giving negative messages over the phone

- allow overlap time for the job sharers
- manage poor performance in a job share sensitively
- make sure your information flows are working well so that all workers have equal access to essential information

But remember, Don't

- offer special terms and conditions to someone as a personal favour
- offer more than you can deliver
- offer terms that leave your customers at a disadvantage
- leave workers unsupervised at home or during flexitime for too long a period

6.4 LEGAL SUMMARY

The statutory rights for part-time and job-sharing staff are covered under the **Employment Protection (Consolidation) Act 1978 as amended, Health and Safety at Work legislation, the Sex and Race Discrimination Acts, and the Equal Pay Act 1970.** A summary of statutory rights is contained in Chapter 7.

There is no legal definition of a part-time contract: it may mean any contract under which the employee works for less than the standard number of hours per week.

The normal hours to accrue continuous employment rights are 16 hours or more a week. This means that protection from unfair dismissal is gained after two years. For those working 8–16 hours a week, it is gained after five years. A recent decision in the House of Lords means that *all* workers in future, regardless of hours worked per week, will be entitled to redundancy pay and to claim unfair dismissal, after two years' service.

Employers are also required by law to consider part-time working for female employees returning from maternity leave if they so request. But the same right does not apply to men.

Part-time staff should be given the same rates of pay, benefits and conditions of service pro-rated to the number of hours worked as full-time staff. They should be treated no less favourably when considering dismissal because of redundancy.

> **Case law**
> The European Court of Justice is at present ruling on three cases of whether a collective agreement is in breach of EEC law if it provides for part-time workers to be paid overtime rates only where they have worked in excess of the normal working hours laid down in the collective agreement.

A recent survey of part-time working in the Industrial Relations Services' Employment Trends found that, in 75% of the organisations surveyed, overtime payments were available to part-timers only once the full-time standard working week had been achieved.

Common law rules about contracts of employment and offers of appointment also apply. See the section on Terms and Conditions of Employment in Chapter 7 for further discussion of legal issues.

The EC Draft Directive on part-time and temporary workers will ensure that part-time workers obtain pro rata rights, health and safety coverage and inclusion in the state insurance system as long as they work 8 hours per week.

7 THE LAW

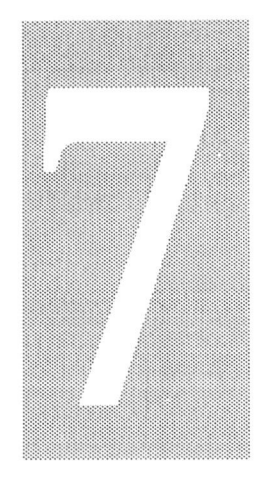

All organisations need to understand their responsibilities under the law and take measures to comply with it. The law is a minimum base of requirements that *have to* be met and from which further action can be taken.

- it is unlawful to discriminate on the grounds of sex, marital status, ethnic group, race, colour, nationality, trade union membership, or being pregnant.

- it is sometimes unlawful to discriminate on the grounds of religion, political belief or being an ex-offender.

- it is not technically unlawful but it is not good practice to discriminate on the grounds of age, sexuality, physical ability or being HIV positive where this is not relevant to doing the job.

Britain, unlike Northern Ireland, does not have legislation that expressly makes religious discrimination unlawful. However, there may be overlaps between racial and religious discrimination. Some religious groups are held to be ethnic groups as defined for the purposes of the Race Relations Act, e.g. Sikhs and Jews, but Rastafarians are not.

EC directives and case law from the European Court of Justice (ECJ) are having an increasing impact on anti-discrimination practice in the UK. They can mean that UK law has to be amended; for example, the EC Pregnant Workers Directive has resulted in the Trade Union Reform and Employment Rights (TURER) Act 1993. Articles of the Treaty of Rome, especially 119 on Equal Treatment, can override gaps and exemptions in the UK laws, and can give direct and enforceable rights to both private and public sector employees.

THE LAW

Each chapter of this handbook includes details of how to comply with the law and of further good practice. This chapter summarises the main parts of the legislation relevant to recruitment, selection and employment.

7.1 THE LAWS COVERED

Disabled Persons Employment Act 1944 and 1958 and (NI) Acts 1945 and 1960 The Companies (Directors' Report) (Employment of Disabled Persons) Regulations 1980, in the Companies Act 1985

Race Relations Act 1976 (does not apply in Northern Ireland)

Equal Pay Act 1970

Sex Discrimination Act 1975 and Sex Discrimination (NI) Order 1976 and amendment

Rehabilitation of Offenders Act 1974 and Exemptions Order 1975

Rehabilitation of Offenders (NI) Order 1978 and Exceptions Order 1979

Trade Union and Labour Relations (Consolidation) Act 1992

Employment Act 1990

Fair Employment (NI) Acts 1976 and 1989

Fair Employment Monitoring Regulations (NI) 1989

Employment Protection (Consolidation) Act 1978 as amended

Contracts of Employment and Redundancy Payments Act [NI] as amended 1965

Trade Union Reform and Employment Rights Act 1993

Access to Medical Reports Act 1988

Access to Medical Records Act 1990

Data Protection Act 1984

EC Directives and ECJ decisions

The full texts of the laws are not reproduced. These and the Home Office guides to the Race Relations Act 1976 and the Sex Discrimination Act 1975 are available from HMSO.

The Codes of Practice on eliminating discrimination and promoting equality of opportunity in employment are available from the Commission for Racial Equality (CRE) and the Equal Opportunities Commission (EOC) respectively. The Code of Good Practice on the Employment of Disabled People is available from the Disablement Advisory Service Team. The Code of Practice on Fair Employment is available from the Fair Employment Commission (FEC). (See the Address section.)

7.2 PEOPLE WITH DISABILITIES

DISABLED PERSONS EMPLOYMENT ACT 1944 AND 1958 AND (NI) ACTS 1945 AND 1960

The Acts established a number of schemes and services to help disabled people into employment.

One of the services is the Register of Disabled Persons, which is maintained by Jobcentres. This is a voluntary register of people who have difficulty in getting or keeping a job because they are seriously handicapped by some kind of health problem or disability. Registration is a requirement for entitlement to some Employment Department schemes — for example, access to special tools or equipment and a grant towards travelling costs to and from work.

People who are registered disabled can also benefit from the quota scheme. This places a duty on employers of more than 20 people to employ a 3% quota of registered disabled people. It is not an offence to be below the quota. However, if an employer is, then they must not engage anyone other than a registered disabled person without first obtaining a permit to do so. Also an employer must not discharge a registered disabled person without reasonable cause if, as a result, they would fall below the quota.

The law technically applies only to larger organisations, but this does not stop small companies taking simple steps in recruitment and employment of people with disabilities.

A new service of Placing, Assessment and Counselling Teams (PACTs) has been set up round the country. PACTs will replace the work of the Disablement Advisory Service, which encouraged employers to improve their policies and practices towards employing people with disabilities. It also helped people with disabilities who are in work to retain their jobs and develop their career potential.

Its work provides a back-up service to that of the Disablement Resettlement Officer (DRO). The DRO's main duties are to provide help to those who need specialist occupational counselling and advice and those who have special needs arising from their disabilities.

THE COMPANIES (DIRECTORS' REPORT) (EMPLOYMENT OF DISABLED PERSONS) REGULATIONS 1980

This is now found in section 235 of and Part III of Schedule 7 to the Companies Act 1985. This places a duty on all UK-registered companies employing an average of more than 250 people to give a policy statement regarding the recruitment, retention, training career development and promotion of people with disabilities in directors' reports.

These regulations relate to policies towards the employment of all disabled workers, including those who are not registered.

The regulations are not applicable to public sector employers or to companies not registered in the UK, but the Department of Employment and the Department of Trade and Industry advise that they should be followed as good practice in all cases.

> **To fulfil this duty you will need to collect detailed information on your workforce. If you are carrying out the recommendations in Chapter 1 on monitoring, then you will have sufficient detail to comply.**

CODE OF GOOD PRACTICE

The Employment Service has published a Code of Good Practice on the Employment of Disabled People (see Chapter 8). This covers:

- deciding on a policy, a section for senior managers
- putting the policy into practice, advice to managers

- descriptions of what disablement may consist of
- an examination of common concerns of employers in the recruitment of people with disabilities
- the recruitment and selection process
- people with disabilities at work
- assisting employees who become disabled
- the role of employees and their representatives
- co-ordination of policy and practice
- help with drawing up a policy
- sources of practical and financial help and advice

GRANTS TO EMPLOYERS OF PEOPLE WITH DISABILITIES

Since April 1994 there has been a new unified scheme of help called 'Access to Work'. This incorporates existing provision but makes some adjustments too. Employers have to make a 50% contribution towards the cost of special equipment costing up to £100. New help will include:

- communication support for deaf people in the workplace
- personal support for people with learning difficulties or severe physical difficulties
- personal support to help people with mental health problems settle in to a job
- adaptations to vehicles

7.3 BLACK AND ETHNIC MINORITY PEOPLE

RACE RELATIONS ACT 1976

This Act makes racial discrimination unlawful in employment, training and related matters, in education, in the provision of goods, facilities and services, and in the disposal and management of premises.

The law applies to everyone but allows certain exemptions: Genuine Occupational Qualifications, positive action and in certain non-employment areas (groups specifically set up to provide charitable services, education, training or welfare services to people in particular racial groups).

THE COMMISSION FOR RACIAL EQUALITY

The 1976 Act set up the Commission for Racial Equality (CRE), whose functions are:

- to work towards the elimination of discrimination
- to promote equality of opportunity and good relations between people of different racial groups
- to keep under review the working of the Act and, when required by the Secretary of State or when it otherwise thinks it necessary, to draw up and submit proposals for amending it.

The CRE also has certain powers to enforce the Act, and issues codes of practice.

DEFINITIONS OF DISCRIMINATION

The Act defined two areas of discrimination:

- *Direct Discrimination* occurs when, on racial grounds alone, a person is treated less favourably than others would be treated in the same circumstances, or is segregated from others.

Making an assumption about the acceptability of employing a person — for example, 'Our clients won't want a black sales worker' — is direct discrimination.

- *Indirect Discrimination* consists of applying, intentionally or unintentionally, a requirement or condition to all people, but it is a requirement

    (i) with which only a 'considerably smaller proportion' of persons in a different racial group can comply,

    (ii) that, irrespective of the colour, race, nationality or ethnic or national origins of the person to whom it is applied, the employer cannot show to be justifiable, and

    (iii) that is to the detriment of that person because they cannot comply with it.

Formal investigations by the CRE have highlighted examples of employment practices that constitute indirect discrimination. For example:

In recruitment and selection, recruitment by word of mouth only and restricting job applicants to people from a particular area

Accepting only British qualifications as evidence of ability or achievement

Specifying a requirement of so many years experience of work in the UK, which could be indirectly discriminatory

Specifying a standard of English higher than is needed for safe and effective performance of the job

Victimisation occurs when a person is less favourably treated because that person has brought discrimination proceedings, given evidence or information in connection with such proceedings, or said that something has been done that would be unlawful under the Act.

Discriminatory practice It is unlawful for an employer to operate a practice that is discriminatory in its effect, even if it has never actually resulted in an act of discrimination.

Other unlawful discrimination Certain other acts are unlawful, including discriminatory advertising, arrangements for job applicants, terms and conditions of service, access to training or promotion, dismissal or redundancy. Giving instructions to a person to discriminate, bringing pressure on a person to discriminate and aiding someone to carry out an unlawful discriminatory act are also unlawful.

In addition, an employer is liable for their employees' discrimination if this occurs in the course of their employment.

POSITIVE ACTION

The Race Relations Act provides for positive action to be taken where particular racial groups are underrepresented in particular work, and to meet special needs.

Positive action describes a range of measures that employers or other persons/bodies can lawfully take to help people from ethnic minorities to compete for jobs on an equal footing with their fellows. (See Chapter 1 for a more detailed discussion of positive action.)

GENUINE OCCUPATIONAL QUALIFICATION

Section 5(2)(d) provides four exemptions to the general rule, whereby you can specifically recruit a person of a particular racial group:

1. where authenticity is required where food or drink is being served

2. when casting parts in a play or other entertainment

3. when employing an artists' model or photographic model

4. when providing those of their racial group with 'personal services promoting their welfare, and those services can most effectively be provided by a person of that racial group'. This provision is most commonly used for social workers, advice workers, etc.

The exemptions are very limited and you have to prove them valid on each case for a particular post. They cannot apply across the board to a group of jobs.

CRE CODE OF PRACTICE

A code of practice for the elimination of racial discrimination and the promotion of equality of opportunity in employment was issued by the CRE and took effect from 1 April 1984. It contains advice on policies and procedures that are needed to prevent discrimination in the recruitment and treatment of employees.

Although the code does not impose any legal obligations, its provisions are admissible in evidence in any proceedings under the Race Relations Act before an industrial tribunal. If employers take the steps that are set out in the code, they may avoid liability for such acts in any legal proceedings brought against them.

> **In other words: It is not the law, but if you don't follow the Code of Practice your case would be in trouble if you ever got taken to a tribunal.**

7.4 SEX DISCRIMINATION

EQUAL PAY ACT 1970

The Equal Pay Act is designed to eliminate discrimination in pay and other terms and conditions of employment, such as bonus payments, holidays and sick leave. It originally provided for equal pay when a man and a woman, working for the same or an associated employer, were doing like work or work judged to be equal by a job evaluation study. However, the Equal Pay Act (Amendment) Regulations significantly extended the Act from 1 January 1984 to provide also equal pay for work of equal value.

> **It is your responsibility to pay the same basic wage to men and women doing the same job in your organisation.**

SEX DISCRIMINATION ACT 1974 & 1986 AND SEX DISCRIMINATION (NI) ORDER 1976 AND AMENDMENT

The Sex Discrimination Act 1975 as amended by the Sex Discrimination Act 1986 and the Employment Act 1989 makes it unlawful to discriminate in respect of employment in Great Britain against a woman (or a man) on the grounds of their sex. Its provisions extend to recruitment, terms and conditions of employment, access to training schemes, opportunities for transfer or promotion, benefits, retirement and dismissal.

Discrimination in employment against a married person because they are married is also an offence.

The law applies to everyone but allows exemptions for groups that are specifically set up to provide charitable services, education, training or welfare services to one sex.

DISCRIMINATION

Discrimination on the grounds of sex is split into two categories as in the Race Relations Act:

- *Direct discrimination* occurs when a person treats a woman, on the grounds of her sex, less favourably than they treat, or would treat, a man

- *Indirect discrimination* consists of applying to a woman a condition or requirement that is the same as for a man but that

    (i) is a condition that only a small number of women would be able to comply with compared with men

    (ii) the employer cannot show to be justified, regardless of whether the condition is applied to men or women, and

(iii) is to the woman's detriment because she cannot comply with it.

For example:
It is unlawful to discriminate against women who are mothers because of their domestic arrangements, or in an interview to ask only women questions about how this would affect their ability to work.

If an employer applies a requirement that all waitresses should wear skirts, even when their performance at work does not depend upon it, this requirement is indirect discrimination if it excludes women who have to wear trousers as part of their religious or cultural practices.

Discrimination against married people It is unlawful to discriminate either directly or indirectly against people because they are married.

Discriminatory practice It is unlawful to operate any practices that would have the effect of discrimination against women even if, in practice, no discrimination has resulted.

Victimisation Anyone who thinks they have been victimised because they have made a complaint under the Act, or have given evidence in such a case, can go to an industrial tribunal.

Other unlawful discrimination Employers are liable for any discriminatory acts done by any person in their employ or acting as their agents unless they can show that they took such steps as were reasonably practicable to prevent the employee or agent from discriminating unlawfully. It is also unlawful to put pressure on another person to perform any discriminatory act.

POSITIVE ACTION

It is permitted for an employer to encourage women to take on a particular type of work if that work at any time during the previous 12 months has been done exclusively or almost exclusively by men. (See Chapter 1 for a longer discussion of positive action.)

GENUINE OCCUPATIONAL QUALIFICATION

The Sex Discrimination Act does not apply when being a woman (or a man) is a genuine occupational qualification for the job. There are very limited circumstances where the GOQ applies. The main occupational qualification used in the voluntary sector is under Section 7(2)(e):

> 'because the nature of the establishment, or that part of it within which the work is done, requires the job to be held by a woman because:
>
> it is a single sex hospital or other establishment, or part of an establishment for persons requiring special care, supervision or attendance; and
>
> - those persons are all women (disregarding the exceptional presence of any man)
>
> - having regard to the essential nature of the establishment, it is reasonable that the job should be held by a woman.'

THE EQUAL OPPORTUNITIES COMMISSION

The Equal Opportunities Commission (EOC) was set up under the Sex Discrimination Act 1975. The Act gives the EOC certain enforcement powers to conduct formal investigations, institute legal proceedings in certain cases and to assist individual complaints in particular circumstances.

EOC CODE OF PRACTICE

A code of practice was issued by the EOC and took effect from 30 April 1985. It contains guidance on how to avoid sex discrimination in recruitment, employment and treatment of employees through policies and procedures. It is concerned with the responsibilities of employers, employees, trade unions and employment agencies.

> **Although the code does not impose any legal obligations, its provisions are admissible in evidence in any proceedings under the Sex Discrimination Act before an industrial tribunal. If employers take steps that are set out in the code, they may avoid liability for such acts in any legal proceedings brought against them.**

7.5 EX-OFFENDERS

REHABILITATION OF OFFENDERS ACT 1974 AND EXEMPTIONS ORDER 1975; REHABILITATION OF OFFENDERS (NI) ORDER 1978 AND EXCEPTIONS ORDER 1979

This Act gives people the right not to reveal certain convictions when these are 'officially spent'. The length of time that must pass before a person's conviction becomes 'spent' in this way depends upon the nature of the sentence and runs from the date of the sentence.

Certain sentences, such as imprisonment, youth custody or corrective training of more than 30 months, can never become spent. A period of imprisonment, youth custody or corrective training of between 6 and 30 months becomes spent after 10 years.

Some professions require applicants to reveal all previous convictions, and there is also a general exception covering all employment that falls into the following categories:

- work involving matters of national security — some civil service posts

- work that brings a person into contact with vulnerable groups, such as the elderly, the infirm, mentally ill people, young people under the age of 18 years, where that person would have access to such minors in the course of their duties

- members of self-regulatory organisations and recognised professional bodies providing financial services and persons directly authorised by the Securities and Investments Board

- certain professions with legal protection, such as nurses or accountants.

EXCEPTED CLASSES OF EMPLOYMENT, OFFICES AND OCCUPATIONS

Judicial appointments
Employment in the office of Director of Public Prosecutions
Employment in the office of the Procurator Fiscal or district court prosecutor or in the Crown Office
Justices' clerks and justices' clerk assistants and their equivalent in Scotland
Constables, police cadets, military, naval and air force police, and certain posts involving police work or assisting the police

Employment in the prison service, including appointment to a Board of Visitors or, in Scotland, to a Visiting Committee,
Traffic wardens
Probation officers
Firearms dealers
Director, controller or manager of an insurance company
Director or manager of a building society
Any occupation concerned with the operation of an abortion clinic or a private hospital or nursing home
Any occupation concerned with the carrying on an establishment for which registration is required by Section 37 of the National Assistance Act 1948 or Section 61 of the Social Work (Scotland) Act
Any occupation for which a certificate of fitness to keep explosives is required
Any occupation requiring a licence, certificate or registration from the Gaming Board of Great Britain
Employment concerned with the provision of health services, within the National Health Service or otherwise, that involves access to patients
Employment concerned with the provision of social services that involves access to the young, the old, the mental or physically less able, or the chronically sick or disabled
Any office or employment concerned with the provision to persons under 18 of accommodation, care, leisure and recreational facilities, schooling, social services, supervision or training, where the holder has access to the young person in the normal course of their duties, which are carried out wholly or partly on the premises where such provision takes place.

Section 43 of the **Banking Act 1979** provides for the exception of employment as a director, controller or manager of a bank, and section 189 of the **Financial**

Services Act provides for the exception of any person employed in certain financial organisations such as Friendly societies, recognised self-regulating organisations and recognised professional bodies.

If the above is not clear, the Home Office will give advice on whether certain jobs are covered by this exemption.

EXCEPTED PROFESSIONS

Medical practitioner
Barrister and advocate
Solicitor
Chartered or certified accountant
Registered teacher (in Scotland)
Nurse, midwife
Pharmaceutical chemist
Opthalmic optician, dispensing optician
Dentist, dental hygienist, dental auxiliary
Any profession to which the **Profession Supplementary to Medicine Act 1960** applies and that is undertaken following registration under that Act.

> **It is your responsibility to make sure that you do not discriminate against those whose convictions are 'spent' in recruitment to jobs that are not covered by the exemptions.**

So you cannot dismiss someone just because you have found out they have a conviction that has been spent, unless they are doing a job covered by these exceptions. A person does not have to disclose 'spent' convictions at interview or on an application form — you have to ask them, and again ask only where the job or profession is covered by the exemptions.

7.6 TRADE UNIONISTS

TRADE UNION AND LABOUR RELATIONS (CONSOLIDATION) ACT 1992, s137 AND EMPLOYMENT ACT 1990 (DOES NOT APPLY IN NORTHERN IRELAND)

Under these Acts it is unlawful to refuse a person employment

1. because they are or are not a member of a trade union, or
2. because they are unwilling to accept a requirement that
   (a) they take steps to become or cease to be or to remain or not to become a member of a trade union, or
   (b) to make deductions or suffer deductions in the event of them not being a member of a union.

A person unlawfully refused employment may make a complaint to an industrial tribunal.

Where an advert is published that indicates or might reasonably be understood as indicating:

(a) that employment to which the advert relates is open only to a person who is or is not a member of a trade union; or
(b) that any requirement as mentioned above will be imposed in relation to employment to which the advertisement relates,

then a person who does not satisfy that condition or is unwilling to accept such a requirement and who seeks and is refused employment to which the advert relates, shall be conclusively presumed to have been refused employment for that reason.

Where there is an arrangement or practice under which employment is offered only to persons put forward or approved by a trade union, and the trade union puts forward or approves only persons who are members of a union, a person who is not a member of the union and who is refused employment in pursuance of the arrangement or practice shall be taken to have been refused employment because they are not a member of the trade union.

Certain employments are excluded:

Members of the armed forces and police service
Employment outside Great Britain
Employment excluded in the interests of national security
Mariners employed on a ship registered outside Great Britain
Share fishermen

Section 137(7) excludes employment or election to an office of a union where union membership is a requirement of the position.

7.7 RELIGIOUS BELIEF OR POLITICAL OPINION (NORTHERN IRELAND)

FAIR EMPLOYMENT (NI) ACTS 1976 AND 1989 AND FAIR EMPLOYMENT MONITORING REGULATIONS (NI) 1989

The purpose of the Fair Employment (NI) Acts 1976 and 1989 is to ensure equality of opportunity in employment in Northern Ireland — for example in applying for a job, gaining promotion, access to training opportunities, dismissal, redundancy, receiving any other work-related benefits — irrespective of religious belief or political opinion.

AIMS AND KEY PROVISIONS OF BOTH ACTS (1976 & 1989)

The 1976 Act had the aim of promoting equality of opportunity and eliminating discrimination.

- *Direct discrimination* is defined as treating a person on religious or political grounds less favourably than others are or would be treated in the same circumstances. The intention or motive of the Respondent to discriminate is not a necessary condition to liability.

- *Indirect discrimination* is defined as applying a requirement or condition that, even without intent, adversely affects considerably more of one religious or political group than another and that can't be justified on non-religious or political grounds.

Discrimination by means of **victimisation** consists of treating a person less favourably than others would be treated in the same cirumstances because that person has made a complaint or allegation of discrimination or has acted as a witness or informant in connection with proceedings under the Acts or has been involved in any other way or intends to do any of those things.

Bodies and organisations other than employers are also prohibited from discriminating, including, for example:

Vocational organisations — trade unions or professional bodies
Persons selecting people for employment by others
Persons for whom work is done under contract
Persons providing training services
Employment agencies and bodies conferring qualifications that are needed for or facilitate employment.

An individual may also suffer sectarian harassment in the workplace, e.g. singing of sectarian songs, sectarian remarks, comments, erection of flags, bunting, etc. This is another form of discrimination and has the effect of intimidating those who suffer from it.

THE KEY PROVISIONS OF THE 1989 ACT

- the establishment of a new Fair Employment Commission and a Fair Employment Tribunal
- the compulsory registration of employers with the Commission
- the compulsory monitoring of workforces and applicants
- the compulsory review by employers of their recruitment, training and promotion practices
- mandatory affirmative action, and the setting of goals and timetables as directed by the Commission
- making indirect discrimination unlawful (direct discrimination had been unlawful since 1976)
- imposition of criminal penalties and economic sanctions for bad practice
- up to £30,000 compensation for individual victims of discrimination
- maintaining by the Commission of a Code of Practice for the promotion of equality of opportunity

The Act places seven key duties on employers:

1. **Registration** All private sector employers with more than 10 employees have to register with the Fair Employment Commission (FEC).

2. **Monitoring** All registered employees, public and private, must monitor the religious composition of their workforces and applicants for employment. All registered employers must make an annual return, based on the results of their findings, to the FEC

3. **Review** All registered employers must formally review their composition and employment practices at least once every three years. The review should cover workplace composition and practices affecting recruitment, training and promotion.

    The purpose of the review is to allow employers to determine whether members of the Protestant or Catholic community are enjoying fair participation in employment. It should also help them to identify appropriate affirmative action.

    The FEC has a duty to give advice to employers about the statutory review when requested to do so.

4. **Affirmative action** Affirmative Action is the key mechanism for change contained in the legislation. Affirmative Action measures are an integral and continuous feature of good employment practice. Affirmative Action measures can be taken voluntarily at any time and are not dependent upon the outcome of a formal interview. During the review, where employers consider that

reasonable and appropriate Affirmative Action could be taken and goals and timetables set, they MUST do so.

5. **Goals and timetables** Goals and timetables for action must be set. They are lawful and consistent with appointment on the basis of merit. They should not be confused with the setting of quotas or the introduction of 'positive' discrimination or reverse discrimination, which are unlawful.

6. **Code of Practice** In carrying out their review, employers must act in regard of the Code of Practice on Fair Employment.

7. **Create a neutral working environment** All employers must prohibit the display of flags, emblems, posters or graffiti, or the circulation of materials, or the deliberate articulation of slogans or songs that are likely to give offence to or cause apprehension among existing or potential employees.

7.8 TERMS AND CONDITIONS OF EMPLOYMENT

EMPLOYMENT PROTECTION (CONSOLIDATION) ACT 1978 AS AMENDED

Under this Act, the following statutory rights are provided:

Statutory rights of employees

Right	Minimum weekly hours	Minimum months employment
Protection from discrimination on grounds of race or sex	None	None
Statement of terms and conditions of employment	16[a]	1
Written particulars must be given by	(8 weeks)	
Right to union membership and to take part in union activities	None	None
Time off work for		
Union duties	16[a]	None
Union activities	16[a]	None
Safety representatives	None	None
Public duties	16[a]	None
Redundant employees	16[a]	24
Ante-natal care	None	None

Right	Minimum weekly hours	Minimum months employment
Maternity leave — right to return[c]	16[a]	24
Statutory maternity pay[c]		
Higher rate	16[a]	24
Lower rate	16[a]	26 weeks
Itemised pay statement	16[a]	None
Notice of termination of employment	16[a]	1
Right not to be unfairly dismissed	8[a]	24[b]
Redundancy pay	8[a]	24
Time off to look for work when redundant	16[a]	24

Notes:

[a] These rights also apply to employees working at least 8 but less than 16 hours per week after five years of continuous service. **However, see page 242 for recent House of Lords ruling on this**.

[b] There is no minimum period of service or weekly hours if the reason for dismissal was sex or race discrimination or was related to the employee's trade union membership or activities.

[c] These rights change in October 1994 — see the TURER Act below

CONTRACTS OF EMPLOYMENT AND REDUNDANCY PAYMENTS ACT (NI) AS AMENDED 1965

This Act specifies terms and conditions of employment in Northern Ireland.

EMPLOYMENT ACT 1990

An employer who makes a spurious offer of employment, defined as an offer that no employer who wanted to fill the post would make, may be subject to litigation.

TRADE UNION (CONSOLIDATION) ACT 1992

This Act makes it unlawful to make an offer of employment subject to membership or non-membership of a trade union.

TRADE UNION REFORM AND EMPLOYMENT RIGHTS ACT 1993

Part 1 of the TURER Act relates to the internal affairs of trade unions, union membership rights and industrial actions.

MATERNITY RIGHTS

Following the EC Directive on Pregnant Workers 92/85, Part II of the Act gives new rights during pregnancy:

- the right of all pregnant workers to 14 weeks' maternity leave — except in cases of suspension on health and safety grounds or where the employee is dismissed during the maternity leave period

- the benefit of the terms and conditions to which she would have been entitled if she had not been absent (apart from pay)

- the right of any worker not to be dismissed for any reason connected with the pregnancy or maternity, and, if dismissed, to have the right to complain to an industrial tribunal regardless of hours of work or length of service

- the right to demand a written statement of the reasons for dismissal regardless of hours worked or length of service if dismissed while pregnant

- the right to be suspended with pay on maternity grounds, if to continue at work would endanger the health and safety of the employee or her baby and no suitable alternative work is available

The Act's provisions on maternity and pregnancy are the first tranche of measures to implement the Directive. Further measures regarding maternity pay and health and safety have yet to be enacted. These provisions must all be enforced by October 1994.

TURER ALSO confers:

- a right to challenge collective agreements terms on the grounds that they are sexually discriminatory (implemented at the end of November 1993) (section 32). This amends section 6 of the 1986 Sex Discrimination Act and allows existing or prospective union members to challenge indirectly discriminatory rules relating to admission or status such as apprenticeship requirements.

- new rules for settling race and sex discrimination out of court
- measures for restricting publicity in tribunal cases involving allegations or sexual harassment and other sexual misconduct (implemented on 30 August 1993) (sections 40 and 41) This amends Schedules 9 and 11 of the 1978 Employment Protection (Consolidation) Act.

MEDICAL RECORDS

The Access to Medical Reports Act 1988 allows a person to have access to a medical report about them if it is prepared by their own doctor. If it is written by a doctor who has not had any responsibility for the care of the person, or by a specialist, then the person does not have a right of access.

When you request a potential employee to have a medical check from their own doctor, the potential employee has the right to see the report. They can ask for it to be amended before being sent to the company or they can have their objections appended if the doctor refuses to amend it.

The doctor cannot submit the report until the person concerned has seen it if they have requested access or until 21 days have passed if they have not requested access.

The Access to Medical Records Act 1990, however, means that an individual can have access to medical *records* held by any medical practitioner (their own or a company doctor or specialist).

REFERENCES

There is no legal obligation to provide a reference. However, if they are given then employers owe a duty to potential employers to provide *accurate references*.

A recent court of appeal decision held that, as a general proposition, a referee holds no duty of care to the subject of the reference. That is, you can give a bad reference if it is still honest and does not defame the person concerned.

7.9 DATA PROTECTION

DATA PROTECTION ACT 1984

The main points in the Act as they affect keeping records or monitoring staff are as follows:

- all employers keeping ethnic or equality records on staff on computer must be registered under the Data Protection Act
- employers must observe the data protection principles of good practice, setting standards for use and accuracy of data
- employers must provide subjects with access to the data and must give employees the opportunity to check data and amend them
- where data are shown to be inaccurate factually then employers can be required to correct or erase data and any recorded opinion based on the inaccurate data

The IPM publishes a Code on Employee Data giving advice on record keeping and handling

7.10 EC DIRECTIVES AND ECJ DECISIONS

PREGNANT WOMEN

DEKKER v. VJV CENTRUM PLUS

This case, recently heard at the European Court of Justice, may have a far-reaching effect on UK employment practice. The Court ruled that it was unlawful sex discrimination to refuse to engage Mrs Dekker in the position of lecturer at the VJV training centre of young adults in Holland because at the time of the interview she was three months pregnant.

The employer is thus denied any opportunity to justify their actions on the economic grounds that they would have to pay two salaries while the woman took maternity leave. To date there is no UK case law, but employers should be aware of the possibility of the unlawfulness of refusing to employ a woman because she is pregnant.

DIRECTIVE ON PREGNANT WORKERS

Most of the measures are contained in TURER. The outstanding issue will be pay provision for the 14 weeks' maternity leave and this will be covered in the Social Security legislation coming in 1994.

FORTHCOMING EC LEGISLATION

DIRECTIVE ON DATA PROTECTION

This is likely to give subjects access to data held on them manually as well as on computer. This has implications for anyone holding paper personnel files that employees do not already have access to.

DIRECTIVE ON PART-TIME AND TEMPORARY WORK

The Commission proposes that part-time and temporary workers should have the same statutory employment protection and social security rights as full-time workers on a pro rata basis.

DIRECTIVE ON WORKING TIME

The draft directive would impose minimum daily and weekly rest periods, minimum annual holiday entitlements with pay, and limits on the hours of work and overtime for night workers. The UK has forced some changes from the Council:

- employees who wish to work more than 48 hours a week can still do so
- people who need or want to work on Sundays can do so
- employers and employees can agree at plant level the arrangements that suit them best.

CHALLENGING PREJUDICE

There are some members of the community who may suffer discrimination but who have no lawful redress should they lose their jobs because of harassment or discrimination at work.

LESBIAN OR GAY WORKERS

Employers are not lawfully obliged at present to ensure a fair employment or selection service to members of the lesbian or gay community, although it looks as if the EC could be taking a lead on this issue.

The EC has agreed to fund a study of the position of gay men and women in Europe following pressure from the International Lesbian and Gay Association. In 1984 the European Parliament passed a resolution on discrimination in the workplace that called for an end to discrimination against lesbians and gay men. However, most member states still discriminate widely.

The following recommendations have been accepted by the EC Civil Liberties Committee, which will press the European Parliament to adopt them:

- appointment of a commissioner responsible for combating homophobia and protecting the fundamental rights of lesbians and gay men
- setting up of a taskforce to prepare a detailed action plan and monitor its implementation
- amendment of the Equal Treatment Directive to include discrimination based on sexual orientation
- review of the Commission's staff regulations with a view to making amendments that would visibly eradicate all forms of discrimination against lesbians and gay men in the workplace

OLDER PEOPLE

There is no legislation covering discrimination on age grounds. As we have seen above, it may constitute indirect discrimination against women to apply an upper age limit. This seems to be the next focus for action from the UK Parliament. There have already been several private members' Bills addressing this issue, and several leading professional bodies have issued statements that they consider applying age criteria an unnecessary and unproductive restriction.

PEOPLE WITH HIV AND AIDS

AIDs is caused by the Human Immunodeficiency Virus (HIV), which attacks the body's natural defence system and leaves it open to various infections. Current medical opinion is that the risk of becoming infected through normal contact at work in most occupations is virtually nil.

If it becomes known that an employee has HIV or AIDs then employers should ensure that the employee can continue to work. If they request to be transferred to less physically demanding work, then that should be facilitated. Discrimination in recruitment or employment should not take place on the grounds that the applicant has HIV or AIDS.

It is particularly important that employers include policies to cover cases where there is no positive lawful protection. It is even more important that these policies are fully implemented and not just paper commitments.

7.11 ACTION SUMMARY

- the most important action to take is to inform yourself of the relevant sections of the law
- send off for the excellent free guides produced by the CRE, EOC and FEC (in Northern Ireland) on advertising, positive action, employment, monitoring and their codes of practice
- visit the local Community Relations Council to discuss your plans

- get in touch with the Disablement Advisory Service and RADAR regarding employment of people with disabilities
- contact LAGER the national organisation that provides information on the employment of lesbians and gay men and a confidential advice service
- contact the APEX Trust about good practice in employing ex-offenders

8 RESOURCES

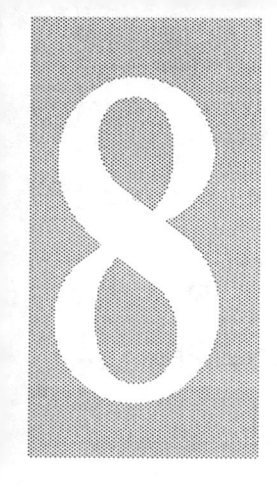

8.1 REFERENCE SECTION

If an organisation is given as the author or publisher, you can write direct for the book — look them up in the Address section.

The Institute of Personnel Management Library publishes a list of Information notes on various topics of interest such as sexual harassment, AIDS and the Workplace, Counselling, etc. Send for the list and an order form to IPM (see Address section).

The Industrial Society publishes a list of publications and training courses, which is available free (see Address section).

EQUAL OPPORTUNITIES

GENERAL POLICY DEVELOPMENT

Developing Equal Opportunity at Work, Margaret Atwood, Employment Relations Resource Centre, 1986 (62 Hills Road, Cambridge, CB2 1LA).

Equal Opportunities — The Way Ahead, Jane Straw, Institute of Personnel Management, 1990.

Equal Opportunities at Work, Mary Coussey and Hilary Jackson, Pitman, 1991.

'The Management of Equal Opportunity', The Rt Hon Baroness Seear, in P. Bramham, E. Rhodes and M. Pearn (eds), **Discrimination and Disadvantage in Employment,** Harper & Row, 1981.

TRAINING, The Implementation of Equal Opportunities at Work, Vols 1 and 2, CRE, 1987.

From Equality to Diversity: A business case for equal opportunities, Rachel Ross and Robin Schneider, Pitman, 1992.

Managing to Discriminate, David Collinson, David Knights and Margaret Collinson, Routledge, 1990.

Maximising Human Resources Through Equal Opportunities, Local Government Management Board, 1990.

Breaking Through the Glass Ceiling, Lesley Abdela, Metropolitan Authorities Recruitment Agency, 1991.

Equal Opportunities Review, journal published six times a year by the Industrial Relations Services, (18–20 Highbury Place, London N5 1QP). Indispensable!

Code of Practice on Equal Opportunities, Institute of Personnel Management.

Equal Opportunities. Ten Point Plan for Employers, Employment Department Group (free from Cambertown Ltd, Employment Department, Goldthorpe Industrial Estate, Goldthorpe, Rotherham, S63 9BC).

BLACK AND ETHNIC MINORITY PEOPLE

Council for Racial Equality, free booklets:

Implementing Equal Opportunity Policies
Equal Opportunity in Employment — A Guide for Employers
Monitoring an Equal Opportunities Policy — A Guide for Employers
Positive Action and Equal Opportunity in Employment
Why Keep Ethnic Records?

Equal Opportunities — WHAT IS POSITIVE ACTION?, Race Relations Employment Advisory Service (11 Belgrave Rd, London SW1H 1RB).

Racial Discrimination and Grievance Procedures — A Practical Guide for Employers, CRE.

Britain's Ethnic Minorities, Trevor Jones, Policy Studies Institute, 1993 (110 Park Village East, London NW1 3SR, 071-387 2171).

PEOPLE WITH DISABILITIES

Code of Practice on the Employment of Disabled People, Employment Service (local job centre).

Recruitment and Retention of People with Disabilities, An Action Checklist, National Federation of Housing Associations, 1988 (175 Gray's Inn Rd, London WC1).

Positive Action towards Employing More People with Disabilities:- Lambeth Council's Experience, London Boroughs' Disability Resource Team, 1988.

Building on Abilities — A Guide for Training People with Disabilities, available from your local Training Agency Operations office.

WOMEN

Women and Men in Britain — A Research Profile, EOC, 1989.

Positive Action: Changing the Workplace for Women, Paddy Stamp and Sadie Robarts, National Council for Civil Liberties.

Women and Employment: A lifetime perspective,
I. Martin and C. Roberts HMSO 1984. (The report of the DE/OPCS 'Women & Employment' Surrey)

Equal Opportunities Commission, free booklets:

Positive Action in Vocational Education and Training
Avoiding Sex Bias in Selection Testing
Equal Opportunities — A Guide for Employers
Fair and Efficient Selection
Guidelines for Equal Opportunities Employers
Positive Action in Recruitment Advertising

WOMEN'S DEVELOPMENT

Springboard. Women's Development Workbook, Liz Willis and Jenny Daisley, Hawthorn Press, 1990.

Women and Power. Gaining back Control, Vida Pearson, PAVIC Publications, 1992.

Train Fair: Women's Training Opportunities Survey, Industrial Society, 1993.

LESBIAN AND GAY PEOPLE

A Hard Hit Community, Savitri Hensman, London Lesbian and Gay Voluntary Sector Network, 1989 (BM Box 5582, London WC1 3XX).

All in a Day's Work. A Report on Anti-lesbian Discrimination in Employment and Unemployment in London, ed. Nina Taylor, Lesbian Employment Rights, 1986 (available from LAGER).

Gay Men at Work, Phil Greasley, Lesbian and Gay Employment Rights, 1986 (available from LAGER).

Less Equal than Others. A Survey of Lesbians and Gay Men at Work (available from Stonewall, 2 Greycoat Place, London SW1P 1SB).

Equal Opportunities for Lesbians and Gay Men: Guidelines to Good Practice in Employment, LAGER, 1993.

EX-OFFENDERS

Releasing the Potential. A guide to good practice for the employment of people with criminal records, Apex Trust, Next Step Training.

Wiping the Slate Clean. An advice leaflet about the Rehabilitation of Offenders Act available from the Home Office, 50 Queen Anne's Gate, London SW1H 9AT.

OLDER PEOPLE

Statement on Age and Employment, Institute of Personnel Management.

CHAPTER 1: EQUALITY TARGETS, POSITIVE ACTION AND MONITORING

Emphasise the Positive — NFCO's Guide to Positive Action for Racial Equality, National Federation of Community Organisations, 1989 (8/9 Upper St, London N1 0PQ, 071 266 0189).

Steps to Racial Equality, Positive Action in a Negative Climate, Elizabeth Burney, Runnymede Research Report, Runnymede Trust 1988 (11 Princelet St, London).

Towards Genuine Consultation — Principles of Community Participation, CRE, 1985.

Positive Action and Equal Opportunity in Employment, CRE, 1991.

Positive Action in Vocational Education and Training, EOC, 1989.

Positive Action in Recruitment and Advertising, EOC, 1989.

Positive Action towards Employing More People with Disabilities:- Lambeth Council's Experience, London Boroughs' Disability Resource Team, 1988.

A Measure of Equality. Monitoring and achieving racial equality in Employment, CRE, 1990.

CHAPTERS 2–4: RECRUITMENT, SELECTION AND APPOINTMENT

Racism and Recruitment, R. Jenkins, Cambridge University Press, 1986.

Employee Selection in the UK, Stephen Bevan and Julie Fryatt, IMS Report No. 160, 1988.

Selection Tests and Sex Bias, A. Pearn and R. D. Mottram, 1988.

Recruitment Code, Institute of Personnel Management.

Code on Occupational Testing, Institute of Personnel Management.

Lines of Progress: An Enquiry into Selection Tests and Equal Opportunities in London Underground, CRE, 1990.

Equal Opportunity Guidelines for Best Test Practice in the Use of Personal Selection Tests, Saville and Holdsworth, 1991 (3 AC Court, High St, Thames Ditton, Surrey T7 0SR).

Guidelines for Testing People with Disabilities, Saville and Holdsworth (as above).

Barriers to Fair Selection, David Collinson, HMSO.

CHAPTER 5: EMPLOYMENT — CONTRACT TERMS AND CONDITIONS

ACAS Guide to Discipline at Work, ACAS.

Croner's Reference Guides. Various handbooks, with an updating service as the law changes, and booklets on key issues such as Grievance; Health and Safety.

GEC Essential Facts, Employment, and The Personnel Manager's Factbook Guides and other handbooks produced and updated by a subscriber service.

Equal Opportunities. Good Employment Practice Pack, Voluntary Action Lewisham (120 Rushey Green, Catford, SE6, 081 695 6000).

Employing People, ACAS, 1985.

Code on Continuous Development, Institute of Personnel Management.

Code on Psychological Testing, Institute of Personnel Management.

Racial Discrimination and Grievance Procedures: A Practical Guide for Employers, CRE.

People, Parity and Pensions. EOC leaflet.

JOB EVALUATION

Understanding Job Evaluation, Mike Burns, Institute of Personnel Management, 1978.

Job Evaluation Schemes Free of Sex Bias, EOC, 1981.

Job Evaluation, ACAS, 1984.

MANAGING CHANGE

Just about Managing — A Guide to Effective Management for Voluntary Organisations and Community Groups, Sandy Adirondack, London Voluntary Service Council, 2nd edn, 1992.

Managing Change in Organisations, Colin Carnall, Prentice Hall, 1990.

HARASSMENT

Women and Harassment at Work, Nathalie Hadjifotiou, Pluto Press, 1984.

Georgie Porgie — Sexual Harassment in Everyday Life, Sue Wise and Liz Stanley, Pandora, 1987.

Sexual Harassment at Work, A TUC Guide for Trade Unionists, TUC, 1983.

Sensitive Issues in the Workplace, Sue Morris, Industrial Society, 1993.

No Offence? Sexual Harassment: How It Happens and How to Beat It, Industrial Society, 1993.

Racial Discrimination and Grievance Procedures, CRE, 1991.

Sexual Harassment — Information Pack, Equal Opportunities Commission.

Preventing and Remedying Sexual Harassment at Work, Michael Rubenstein, Industrial Relations Services, 1992.

Sexual Harassment in the Workplace — The Facts Employees Should Know, Department of Employment, 1992.

Bullying at Work: How to Confront and Overcome It, Andrea Adams, Virago, 1992.

Statement on Harassment, Institute of Personnel Management.

CHAPTER 6: FLEXIBLE WORKING

Job Sharing; Employment Rights and Conditions, New Ways to Work.

The Legal Context of Job Sharing, New Ways to Work.

Fair Shares: Making Job Shares Work, Mike Rosen and Patricia Leighton, Hackney Job Share, 1991 (380 Old St, London EC1V 9LT.

Flexibility and Choice — New Work Patterns for the Nineties, Local Government Management Board, 1993.

New Work Patterns, Patricia Leighton and M. Syrett, Pitman, 1989.

CHAPTER 7: THE LAW

Discrimination Law, Michael Malone, Kogan Page, 1993.

CRE, free booklets:

Positive Action and Equal Opportunity in Employment
Guidelines for Advertisers and Employers — Race Relations Act 1976
Monitoring an Equal Opportunities Policy
Why Keep Ethnic Records?

EOC, free booklets:

Positive Action in Vocational Education and Training
Guidelines for Equal Opportunities Employers
Positive Action in Recruitment Advertising
Pregnancy and the Sex Discrimination Act
The Sex Discrimination Act and Advertising
Equal Pay — A Guide to the Equal Pay Act

Sex and Race Discrimination in Employment, Camilla Palmer and Kate Poulton, Legal Action Group, 1987 (242 Pentonville Rd, London N1).

Racial Discrimination — A Guide to the Race Relations Act 1976, Home Office.

Sex Discrimination — A Guide to the Sex Discrimination Act 1975, Home Office.

Code of Practice for the Elimination of Discrimination on the Grounds of Sex and Marriage and the Promotion of Equality of Opportunity in Employment, EOC, 1985.

Code of Practice for the Elimination of Racial Discrimination and the Promotion of Equality of Opportunity in Employment, CRE, 1983.

The Handbook of Race Discrimination, Harjit Grewal, Sphere, 1988.

8.2 ADDRESS SECTION

GENERAL RESOURCING ORGANISATIONS

Industrial Relations Services
18–20 Highbury Place
London
N5 1QP
071–354 5858
Produces *Equal Opportunities Review* and other publications and conferences on equal opportunities issues

Industrial Society
Robert Hyde House
48 Bryanston Square
London
W1H 7LN
071-262 2041
Campaigns, researches, trains, provides consultancy on employment, management and equal opportunities

Institute of Personnel Management
IPM House
Camp Road
Wimbledon
London
SW19 4UW
081-946 9100
Produces resources on personnel and salary setting

Local Government Management Board
Arndale House
Arndale Centre
Luton
LU1 2TS
0582 451166
Researches and produces reports on issues for local government

Policy Studies Institute
110 Park Village East
London
NW1 3SR
071-387 2171
Independent research organisation in economics, social policy and the workings of political institutions

TUC Equality and Social Policy Dept
Congress House
Great Russell St
London
WC1B 3LS
071-636 4030
Provides useful publications on equal rights and social, health and environmental protection issues

EQUAL OPPORTUNITIES — GENERAL

Commission for Racial Equality
10–12 Allington St
London
SW1
071-828 7022
Produces guides to the Race Relations Act and many books and leaflets, and can provide advice on employment and discrimination issues

Institute of Race Relations
247–9 Pentonville Rd
London
N1 9NG
071-837 0041
Provides information and publishes books and resources

Runnymede Trust
11 Princelet Street
London
E1 6QH
071–375 1496
Has a resource library and produces books and the journal *Race and Immigration* (which has a very useful source section) ten times a year

PEOPLE WITH DISABILITIES

Disability Alliance
25 Denmark St
London
WC2H 8NJ
071-240 0806
Campaigns for better employment and benefit rights for people with disabilities.

Connections Partnership
94 Howard Road
Leicester
LE2 1XH
0533 705876
Contact: Gill Taylor

Disabled Living Foundation
380–384 Harrow Rd
London
W9 2HG
081-289 6111
Provides information on employing people with disabilities

The Employment Service
Rockingham House
123 West St
Sheffield
S1 4ER
Distributes the Code on Employment of Disabled People

Greater London Association of Disabled People
336 Brixton Rd
London
SW9 7AA
071-274 0107
Provides leaflets, directories, regular newsletters and other information for disabled people in London

RADAR
25 Mortimer St
London
W1N 8AB
071-637 5400

PEOPLE OF DIFFERENT RELIGIONS AND POLITICAL PERSUASIONS IN NORTHERN IRELAND

Fair Employment Commission
Andras House
60 Great Victoria St
Belfast
BT2 7BB
0232 240020
Advice on and enforcement of Fair Employment Act Northern Ireland

WOMEN

Equal Opportunities Commission
Overseas House
Quay Street
Manchester
M3 3HN
061-833 9244
Produces guides to the Sex Discrimination Act and information on employment rights, and can give advice

Maternity Alliance
15 Britannia St
London
WC1X 9JP
071-837 1265
Campaigns for better maternity rights for all women

National Childcare Campaign
Wesley House
79 Great Queen St
London
WC2B 5AX
071-405 5617
Campaigns for better maternity rights for all women

LESBIAN AND GAY PEOPLE

Lesbian and Gay Employment Rights (LAGER)
St Margaret's House
21 Old Ford Rd
London
E2 9PL
081-983 0696
Produces regular bulletins on lesbian and gay employment rights and issues and can give advice to individuals facing discrimination at work

EX-OFFENDERS

Apex Trust
2–4 Colchester St
London
E1 7PG
071-481 4831
Advice and consultancy on all issues regarding the employment and recruitment of ex-offenders

NACRO
169 Clapham Rd
London
SW9
071-582 6500
NACRO is the organisation for the care and resettlement of offenders and can advise on employment rights for ex-offenders. It has many local projects.

AIDS AND HIV RESOURCE ORGANISATIONS

Employment Medical Advisory Services
Has a network of doctors and nurses available for free advice to employers and employees

Health Education Council
78 New Oxford St
London
WC1 1AH
Produces booklets and gives information

Terence Higgins Trust
BM/AIDS
London
WC1N 3XX
071-833 2971
Produces free information and telephone advice and counselling

THE LAW AND EMPLOYMENT ISSUES

ACAS
27 Wilton St
London
SW1X 7AZ
071-210 3000
The Employment Department and ACAS produce leaflets on employment rights

Department of Social Security
Alexander Fleming House
London
SE1 6BY
071-407 5522
Produces many free guides and leaflets on individual's employment rights.

Employment Department
Caxton House
Tothill St
London
SW1H 9NF
071-273 3000

Women in Management
64 Marryat Rd
London
SW19 5BN
081-944 6332
Promotion and development of women into management

Women Returners' Network
c/o Ruth Michaels
Hatfield Polytechnic
College Lane
Hatfield
Herts
Keeping in touch with other returners

JOB SHARING

Data Protection Registrar
Wycliffe House
Water Lane
Wilmslow
Cheshire
0625 535777

New Ways to Work
347a Upper St
London
N1
071-226 4026
Advises on job-sharing arrangements and terms and conditions